DISCIPLINED ENTREPRENEURSHIP
WORKBOOK

DISCIPLINED ENTREPRENEURSHIP
WORKBOOK

BILL AULET

Illustrations by
Marius Ursache

Edited by
Chris Snyder

Published by John Wiley & Sons, Inc., Hoboken, New Jersey
Published simultaneously in Canada

For general information about our other products and services, please contact our Customer Care Department within the United States at (800) 762-2974, outside the United States at (317) 572-3993 or fax (317) 572-4002.

Wiley publishes in a variety of print and electronic formats and by print-on-demand. Some material included with standard print versions of this book may not be included in e-books or in print-on-demand. If this book refers to media such as a CD or DVD that is not included in the version you purchased, you may download this material at http://booksupport.wiley.com. For more information about Wiley products, visit www.wiley.com.

Library of Congress Cataloging-in-Publication Data has been applied for and is on file with the Library of Congress.

978-1-119-36579-2 (paperback)
978-1-119-36577-8 (ePDF)
978-1-119-36578-5 (ePUB)

Printed in the United States of America

SKY10034202_042222

I DEDICATE THIS BOOK TO ALL MY STUDENTS WHO MAKE MY SO-CALLED "JOB"
THE GREATEST ONE IN THE WORLD. YOU GIVE ME ENERGY EVERY DAY. THIS ONE IS FOR YOU.

CONTENTS

STEP 3

Build an End User Profile for the Beachhead Market **47**

What Is Step 3, Build an End User Profile for the Beachhead Market?
Why Do We Do This Step, and Why Do We Do It Now?
Process Guide
General Exercises to Understand Concept
Worksheet

STEP 4

Estimate the Total Addressable Market (TAM) for the Beachhead Market **53**

What Is Step 4, Estimate the Total Addressable Market (TAM) for the Beachhead Market?
Why Do We Do This Step, and Why Do We Do It Now?
Process Guide
General Exercises to Understand Concept
Worksheets
Advanced Topics: Bottom-Up TAM Analysis

STEP 5

Profile the Persona for the Beachhead Market **65**

What Is Step 5, Profile the Persona for the Beachhead Market?
Why Do We Do This Step, and Why Do We Do It Now?
Process Guide
General Exercises to Understand Concept
Worksheets
Advanced Topic: Persona Profiles for Multisided End User Market

STEP 6

Full Life Cycle Use Case **79**

What Is Step 6, Full Life Cycle Use Case?
Why Do We Do This Step, and Why Do We Do It Now?
Process Guide
General Exercises to Understand Concept
Worksheets

STEP 7

High-Level Product Specification **87**

What Is Step 7, High-Level Product Specification?
Why Do We Do This Step, and Why Do We Do It Now?
Process Guide
General Exercises to Understand Concept
Worksheets
Advanced Topic: High-Level Product Brochure

STEP 8

Quantify the Value Proposition **95**

What Is Step 8, Quantify the Value Proposition?
Why Do We Do This Step, and Why Do We Do It Now?
Process Guide
General Exercises to Understand Concept
Worksheets

STEP 9

Identify Your Next 10 Customers 101

What Is Step 9, Identify Your Next 10 Customers?
Why Do We Do This Step, and Why Do We Do It Now?
Process Guide
General Exercises to Understand Concept
Worksheets

STEP 10

Define Your Core 113

What Is Step 10, Define Your Core?
Why Do We Do This Step, and Why Do We Do It Now?
Process Guide
General Exercise to Understand Concept
Worksheet

STEP 11

Chart Your Competitive Position 119

What Is Step 11, Chart Your Competitive Position?
Why Do We Do This Step, and Why Do We Do It Now?
Process Guide
General Exercise to Understand Concept
Worksheet

STEP 12

Determine the Customer's Decision-Making Unit (DMU) 125

What Is Step 12, Determine the Customer's Decision-Making Unit (DMU)?
Why Do We Do This Step, and Why Do We Do It Now?
Process Guide
General Exercises to Understand Concept
Worksheet

STEP 13

Map the Process to Acquire a Paying Customer 131

What Is Step 13, Map the Process to Acquire a Paying Customer?
Why Do We Do This Step, and Why Do We Do It Now?
Process Guide
General Exercises to Understand Concept
Worksheets

BONUS TOPIC

Windows of Opportunity and Triggers 143

What Are Windows of Opportunities and Triggers?
Why Are They Important and Why Now?
Process Guide
General Exercises to Understand Concept
Worksheet

PREFACE

THE ORIGINAL *DISCIPLINED ENTREPRENEURSHIP* book laid out a rigorous but practical pedagogy for innovation-driven entrepreneurship. It has fundamentally changed the course of entrepreneurship education from a storytelling approach to a toolbox and systematic framework. But there is only so much that can be accomplished in a single 250-page book. This workbook builds off *Disciplined Entrepreneurship* to provide a way to more easily engage with the 24 Steps.

Our goal at the Martin Trust Center for MIT Entrepreneurship is to develop high-quality entrepreneurship education and make it accessible, not just to MIT's full-time students but also to millions of people worldwide. That is why I wrote *Disciplined Entrepreneurship*, taught several online courses on edX, and with my colleagues write online articles and tools to help clarify key concepts about our methodical approach to entrepreneurship.

The demand from entrepreneurs and instructors for additional materials to help them implement the 24 Steps has been simultaneously rewarding and overwhelming. There needed to be a more scalable solution, and that is the purpose of this workbook.

In this book, I provide templates and additional advice on how to implement each of the 24 Steps. You can use these templates on your own startup or as classroom deliverables to assess your students' understanding of the topics. This workbook is not a replacement for *Disciplined Entrepreneurship* but rather a complement to it. It is expected that you will go back and forth between *Disciplined Entrepreneurship* and this workbook in order to gain a full understanding of each step.

The 24 Steps is an iterative process, so always make sure you are proactively revising your work as you go through the steps. Something that you do in Step 23 is likely to affect Step 11, or Step 9 will affect Step 5, and so on. Also, do not feel confined by these templates if you need to make some modifications to better suit the needs of the industry or specific characteristics of your startup.

The 24 Steps approach is a toolbox of the best methodologies available for entrepreneurs, and I continually evolve it and survey the landscape to take in new and/or better tools to improve the framework. You'll see two new chapters in this workbook, one on primary market research and another on windows of opportunity and triggers. I hope that many others around the world will continue to test and contribute to the 24 Steps to make the framework even better over time. The collective wisdom of the community is better than any individual—plus many hands make for lighter and faster work.

Since the time I first published *Disciplined Entrepreneurship*, it has become even more clear that we need high-quality, rigorous entrepreneurship education and training sooner rather than later. The critical need for a serious body of knowledge on innovation-driven entrepreneurship has never been greater—and it will only get more so in the future. Please "lean in," as Sheryl Sandberg would say, and help us with this cause.

Additional materials, including electronic versions of some of the worksheets herein, will be available at www.disciplinedentrepreneurship.com.

INTRODUCING THE DISCIPLINED ENTREPRENEURSHIP CANVAS

THIS IS NEW MATERIAL that was not covered in *Disciplined Entrepreneurship*. The Canvas is a tool you will fill out as you go through the 24 Steps.

WHAT IS THE DISCIPLINED ENTREPRENEURSHIP CANVAS, AND WHY IS IT IMPORTANT?

The Disciplined Entrepreneurship Canvas is a one-page overview of the Disciplined Entrepreneurship approach to entrepreneurship. The Canvas functions like a synopsis of your current status so you can see what you have done and what you have not done, across 10 major areas that map to the 24 Steps.

I have seen the value in life of having a concise visual that gives a team feedback on their progress in the midst of the battle. I have also seen entrepreneurs building workarounds for just this function when trying to use the Disciplined Entrepreneurship approach, so there is clearly value in tracking your progress on the long journey through the 24 Steps.

The Disciplined Entrepreneurship Canvas will allow you to quickly assess the big picture of where you stand, and where your strengths and weaknesses are, so you can make adjustments.

HOW TO APPROACH THE DISCIPLINED ENTREPRENEURSHIP CANVAS

As Disciplined Entrepreneurship has been broadly deployed, a frequent question I get is how to integrate the 24 Steps framework with the Business Model Canvas made popular by *Business Model Generation* by Alexander Osterwalder and Yves Pigneur. In fact, before I wrote *Disciplined Entrepreneurship*, I used to use in my classroom the Business Model Canvas and then the Lean Canvas by Ash Maurya, but I did not find an easy, suitable way to integrate them with teaching the 24 Steps.

As nature abhors a vacuum, numerous people have constructed their own canvases for the Disciplined Entrepreneurship framework, led by Laurie Stach (MIT Launch), Floriano Bonfigli (Istituto Adriano Olivetti Business School—ISTAO Startup Lab), Patrick Kirby (Michelin—vice president of innovation and entrepreneurship), Johannes Mutzke (Michelin—Global Innovation Council), Mateo Nakach and Jorge Sanchez (Build-Your-Business Consulting Group), and Michael McCausland (Leadership Institute for Entrepreneurs).

They have pushed and inspired me to see the value of a one-page canvas that shows how you are doing. In sports, a coach often tracks progress in the game in a summary fashion and then conveys key information to his team on what they are doing well and what they need to focus more on if they are to win the game. A basketball coach's synopsis, for instance, will not only have the score but also the time left in the game, how many fouls each team and each player has, and other key indicators. Likewise, an entrepreneurship canvas gives you the big picture in one snapshot and allows you to see what you need to work on.

The simple summary does not capture the full richness of your situation, and as such it is not a perfect indicator of your success. Nor does the simple summary tell you why things have happened and how to fix things. So while it is limited in its usefulness, it does have the benefit of simplicity.

I have based the Disciplined Entrepreneurship Canvas off the Six Themes of the 24 Steps from *Disciplined Entrepreneurship*, expanding two of the themes and adding two more sections. The resulting Canvas maintains the specificity, logic, and rigor of the 24 Steps.

More so than other canvases, this canvas has a suggested initial sequential nature to it. You should start with Section 1 and then follow the arrows to move through the canvas. There should also be iteration, but providing a general prescriptive initial flow is helpful and an important part of the Disciplined Entrepreneurship approach.

Turn to page xviii to see the Canvas. Each section maps quite well to specific steps:

Section 1, Raison d'Être (aka Reason for Existing): Step 0

Section 2, Initial Market: Steps 1, 2, 3, 4, 5, and 9

Section 3, Value Creation: Steps 6, 7, and 8

Section 4, Competitive Advantage: Steps 10 and 11

Section 5, Customer Acquisition: Step 12, 13, and Windows of Opportunity/Triggers

Section 6, Product Unit Economics: Steps 15, 16, 17, and 19

Section 7, Sales: Step 18

Section 8, Overall Economics: Step 19 (parts)

Section 9, Design and Build: Steps 20, 21, 22, and 23

Section 10, Scaling: Steps 14 and 24

The fit between the steps and the Canvas is not perfect, but it still produces a framework that is useful and ties into the worksheets and additional information in this workbook.

When I used other canvases in my classroom, the frameworks were helpful, but they often needed to be customized. I would likewise encourage you to think of the Disciplined Entrepreneurship Canvas below not as a fixed edict, but rather as a framework that can be customized as appropriate. If it does not quite fit, that is okay. Go ahead and customize it, but it should at least give you a good start.

Note: Filling out the Disciplined Entrepreneurship Canvas fully requires expertise that you will gain from reading both *Disciplined Entrepreneurship* and this workbook. Do not be discouraged or frustrated that you don't know how to fill out all the sections at first. It will be a good guide for you to make sure you have absorbed all the material in both books. Fill out what you can and then continually update it as you learn more.

EXAMPLE OF USING THE DISCIPLINED ENTREPRENEURSHIP CANVAS WITH FEEDBACK

Old friend and master illustrator of this book, Marius Ursache, offered to test-drive the Canvas for his project, the Disciplined Entrepreneurship Toolbox (www.detoolbox.com). I should note that the 24 Steps framework has been used not just for startups but for projects/product design and development in large corporations, government organizations, investment situations, community organizations, educational institutions, religious groups, student clubs, and even creative arts groups. Once it was used for a piano concert. (Thanks for letting us know, Amanda von Goetz!)

Turn to page xix to see his first draft of his Canvas. Below are my comments on it so that you can see what you should be considering when you fill out your Canvas. Marius's draft is quite good, so I will focus my comments on where it could be improved, as well as how the Canvas will help Marius discover where he should focus his attention next:

1. **Raison d'Etre**: The founder passions, values, initial assets, and initial idea are good and can be refined, but the real area I would focus on is the mission. It is too general and is not really unique or inspiring. Having a clear mission is valuable for two reasons—it shows why the world will be a better place thanks to your venture, and equally important, it tells you what you will *not* be doing. This guidance on what you will be not doing will help you to get the right people on your team. To build a successful team you need three things: a common vision, shared values, and complementary skills. As you can see, it starts with common vision, so clarity on why you are in business is fundamental to your success in an environment that will be fraught with failure and other discouraging moments. That common vision keeps you marching on.

2. **Initial Market**: Again, there is lots to like in the End User Profile, TAM, and Next 10 Customers. The Beachhead Market and Persona draw my attention and concern. First, I worry that the Beachhead Market is two different markets. There cannot be a plural of Beachhead Market. Second, I worry even more that there is no Persona. I know picking a Persona can be a bit

The Disciplined Entrepreneurship Canvas

PRODUCT _____ REVISION _____ DATE _____

① Raison d'Être
Why are you in business?

Mission:

Passion:

Values:

Initial Assets:

Initial Idea:

② Initial Market
Who is your customer?

Beachhead:

End User Profile:

TAM:

Persona:

First 10 Customers:

③ Value Creation
What can you do for your customer?

Use Case:

Product Description:

Problem Being Solved:

Quantified Value Proposition:

④ Competitive Advantage
Why you?

Moats:

Core:

Competitive Positioning:

⑤ Customer Acquisition
How does your customer acquire your product?

DMU:

Process to Acquire Customer:

Windows of Opportunity:

Possible Triggers:

⑥ Product Unit Economics
Can you make money?

Business Model:

Estimated Pricing:

Short Term LTV:
Short Term COCA:
Medium Term LTV:
Medium Term COCA:
Long Term LTV:
Long Term COCA:

⑦ Sales
How do you sell your product

Preferred Sales Channel:

Sales Funnel:

Short Term Mix:

Medium Term Mix:

Long Term Mix:

⑧ Overall Economics
Does your product make money?

Estimated R&D Expenses:

Estimated G&A Expenses:

LTV/COCA Ratio High Enough:

⑨ Design & Build
How do you produce the product?

Identify Key Assumptions:

Test Key Assumptions:

MVBP:

Tracking Metrics:

⑩ Scaling
How do you scale your business?

Product Plan for Beachhead:

Next Market:

Product Plan beyond Beachhead:

Follow-on TAM:

The Disciplined Entrepreneurship Canvas

PRODUCT: DE Toolbox   **REVISION:** 1.0   **DATE:** October 20, 2016

1 Raison d'Être
Why are you in business?

Mission: Help more startups around the world to become successful, and improve lives, fix unemployment, and grow economies. Help more people to invest in startups in a smart way.

Founder passions: Startups and innovation, teaching, interacting with smart people.

Values: transparent, competitive, fair play.

Initial Assets: Team (Marius & Vlad), connections (Bill Aulet, MIT, accelerators), current users (5,000+ for current product).

Initial Idea: Online tool to help startups accelerate and get funded.

2 Initial Market
Who is your customer?

Beachhead Market:
A. Early-stage founders who want to improve their startup's chances to fundraise.
B. Accelerators outside Silicon Valley who want to improve their process and outcomes.

End User Profile:
A. Tech founders outside major US startup hubs with an idea or product but no revenue.
B. Smaller accelerators who have trouble getting good deals and accelerating them properly.

TAM: 1M tech founders outside US ($100M). 5,000 smaller accelerators ($30M).

Persona: TBD

10 Customers: MVP Academy (RO), NUMA (FR), MITEF Poland (PL), IncubatecUFRO (CL), UDD Ventures (CL), Magical Startups (CL), Eleven (BG), HUStart (IL), MadeInJLM (IL), AccelerateKorea (KR).

3 Value Creation
What can you do for your customer?

Use Case:
A. Learn about the biz side of your startup, apply it using a vetted process (DE24) & online tools.
B. Recruit better startups, engage more mentors, accelerate startups faster, get them funded.

Product Description: Process & toolbox for founders & accelerators—marketplace.

Problem:
A. Founders lack guidance and tools to help them be more disciplined on the business side.
B. Accelerators' "spray and pray" strategy does not yield too many successful startups.

Quantified Value Proposition:
A. Move faster. Get funded faster.
B. Get better deals. Get better follow-on investments for startups.

4 Competitive Advantage
Why you?

Moats: Network effect (both startups/accelerators use it).

Core: We match the best startups with the best accelerators/investors, and help them work smarter together.

Competitive Positioning: Better productivity than AngelList, F6S. Focused on process more than Visible, FounderSuite, Gust.

5 Customer Acquisition
How does your customer acquire your product?

Decision Making Unit:
A. Founders & Chief Product Officers
B. Sponsor: CIO/CTO or Managing Director of accelerator. Decision: managing team.

Decision Making Process:
A. Start trial, share with team, add data, discuss with team before trial expiration.
B. Analyze features & cost for tools, contact suppliers, negotiate & sign (4-6 mo).

WoOs:
A. Apply to accelerator, prepare for fundraising
B. New generation/new fund (twice per year) or change in leadership

Possible Triggers:
B. Discounts, sales rep meetings or events.

6 Product Unit Economics
Can you make money?

Business Model: Subscription model for both startups & accelerators.

Pricing: $15/mo per startup

Short term LTV: $200 / $15,000
Short term COCA: $10 / $2,000

Medium term LTV: $250 / $25,000
Medium term COCA: $7 / $1,750

Long term LTV: $275 / $32,000
Long term COCA: $5 / $1,500

7 Sales
How do you sell your product

Preferred Sales Channel:
A. Website
B. Direct sales

Sales Funnel:
A. Search online→Read features & testimonials →Create trial→Add data in app→Receive trial end email→Discuss with team→Buy.
B. Search tools/get referrals→Analyze features→Discuss with sales reps→Discuss with team→Negotiate→Sign contract→Buy.

Short Term Mix: Email newsletter, event presentations, inbound, direct sales.

Medium/Long Term Mix: Event presentations, inbound, direct sales.

8 Overall Economics
Does your product make money?

Est R&D Exp: $50,000

Est G&A Exp: $24,000

LTV/COCA Ratio: 20:1 / 7:1

9 Design & Build
How do you produce the product?

Key Assumptions:
1. Startups will use the tool recurrently.
2. Accelerators need a better tool to source startups (than F6S/AngelList/Google Forms) and manage the acceleration process (than Google Docs/Slack/Email).

Assumption Tests:
1. Simplify tool (not linear, iterative/depth)
2. Try selling a prototype/slideware.

MVBP:
1. Current product with subscription
2. Presentation/prototype for accelerator features

Tracking Metrics:
1. Retention for startups
2. Number of paying startups
3. Number of paying accelerators

10 Scaling
How do you scale your business?

Product Plan for BHM: ???

Next Market: Universities, Angel groups

Product plan beyond BHM: Marketplace

Follow-on TAM: 100,000 angels ($1B).

uncomfortable and you will not find the perfect one to start, but Marius should pick the best one he has and then execute the process with it and look to upgrade the Persona over time.

3. **Value Creation**: There is a great deal of information to be summarized in this box and it is a real challenge. I worry that the very important use case is so truncated that it is not clear how well this has been developed. Likewise, the other three items have to be summarized in such a compact way, so while they seem encouraging I have a lot of questions. I definitely want to see the product brochure. But all in all, good. At this point, I am starting to see that the two Beachhead Markets defined in the Initial Market section *may* be intractably linked, and rather than two separate markets, they could *possibly* be seen as a two sided-market. This would be an area I would ask a lot of questions about.

4. **Competitive Advantage**: In the moats section, Marius lists "network effect," but I think that is actually the Core. What Marius lists for the Core definitely is not a Core, but rather is the benefit that customers will get. A Core is an internal capability you will have that is unique or much stronger than anyone else. I worry when I see network effect as a Core because while it can be a great one, it is rarely achieved. And if is not achieved, then the company has no defensible advantage over others, who will be able to follow you into the market at a lower cost by learning from the first mover's mistakes.

5. **Customer Acquisition**: The Decision-Making Unit (DMU) seems to be to be too simplistic (although I like that he has identified the chief product officer). Who are the DMU's primary influencers? The Decision-Making Process is too simplistic and does not address creating awareness with the target market enough. The windows of opportunity are a good start, but the possible triggers section is not developed in any creative way. This section, like much of the Canvas (and like what I'd expect for a first pass on any canvas), is too general and lacking in specifics to this situation.

6. **Product Unit Economics**: I like that these are general estimates and that they do not try to convey a level of precision that is not attainable at this point. The short-term Cost of Customer Acquisition (COCA) of $10 seems absurdly low to me and I am confident that upon closer evaluation, Marius will find this number to be much higher, which is expected in the short term. It would be extremely unusual to see a short-term Lifetime Value (LTV) of $200 with only a short-term COCA of $10, or a short-term LTV of $15,000 with a short term COCA of only $2,000. This immediately makes me discount the medium term and long term where I am confident that the COCA is still too low. But if the LTVs are to be believed, the business will be able to handle the actual COCA. Notice how easy it is to get a sense of the business from just a few numbers!

7. **Sales**: Oh my goodness! With the very low COCA from the previous section, I expected to see no direct sales channel utilization in this section (forgoing direct sales is risky in the short term), but there it is as the second option. He'll really need to think about how to minimize use and cost of direct sales (likely use inside sales instead of field sales, for starters) and to use other sales methods to keep COCA down. Maybe he can do online chat sales early on so that inside sales is more affordable. I think "robo-sales" using big data analysis and preference engines is probably the way to go. I am feeling even less confident about the COCA calculations now, and I would dig deeper to make sure the unit economics model gets refined. The mentality of the organization needs to be more focused on designing the sales process to have no human interaction from the company's side in the near future, so that the COCA does not grow out of control.

8. **Overall Economics**: The R&D expense and the G&A expense items seem reasonable since the work is being done in Romania, not the United States, but the LTV/COCA ratio still bothers me because I think the actual COCA is higher. However, this part of the Canvas shows me that if the LTV is accurate, there is room for the COCA to be higher and still have an economically sustainable and attractive business entity.

9. **Design & Build**: The key assumptions are too few and too general. The assumption tests do not yet line up with the key assumptions. The Minimum Viable Business Product (MVBP) is already up and running, so there is valuable information that can be gained from this investment so far. The tracking metrics are generally correct, but are also more general than I would like to see; for example, they do not have a time frame indicated.

10. **Scaling**: What Marius put here is very general, but that is not as much a problem as it would be in the other sections, because you won't have much clarity this early on. That being said, Marius should keep an eye on this section going forward and update it quarterly based on new information, which will be coming in as he engages in the market and learns from iterations on earlier steps.

STEP 0

How Do I Get Started? Should I?

Before you start this 24-step journey, you first want to know two things:

1. Do I want to start a company?
2. Do I have an idea or technology that I can do a Market Segmentation on (Step 1)?

Starting a company is not easy—it's the exact opposite. It will be really, really difficult and humbling throughout the journey. So do you really want to start a company? How do you optimize your chances of reaching a satisfying reward at the end? What kind of preparation do you need so that you start out with your eyes wide open, fully understanding what a startup entails and having done everything you can to increase your odds of success?

By the Book: See pages 15-21 of Disciplined Entrepreneurship for basic knowledge on this step.

I have a
technological
breakthrough!

I have
an idea!

I have
a passion!

Three ways
to start a new venture

In Step 0 of *Disciplined Entrepreneurship*, I said that people interested in entrepreneurship typically either have an idea, a technology, or a strong interest in entrepreneurship. I discussed how someone without an idea or technology can think about what knowledge and skills they have and what ideas/technologies might flow from there.

Here, I emphasize unequivocally that if you're looking to radically impact the world, you need not just an idea or technology, but you also need a passion to keep going through good times and bad. You'll also need cofounders who can help round out the skills and knowledge leading the company. MIT's research shows that solo founders struggle compared to startups with founding teams.[1]

In this workbook, I'll first walk you through exercises to assess and define your starting point so that you are better equipped to determine whether and how you want to proceed.

YOUR PASSION

I start with passion because if you don't have this, you will never succeed. It is a necessary condition (you must have it) but not a sufficient one (you need other things, too). Without passion, when you hit those tough times—and you will, without question—you will not be able to fight through.

By definition, a startup is about doing something that has never been done before. You are experimenting every day in new terrain, and you and your team will be way out of your comfort zone. You and they must be. It is all so new. You hope to succeed, but you will fail, in ways big and small, and often. Failed experiments are part of the startup experience. Just like in sports, where no great player has ever made all the shots he takes nor won every game she plays, you will do a lot of things that don't work right away, or don't work at all. You have to have a passion to fight through these temporary setbacks.

Passion Checklist

	I understand that...	Yes	No
1	Founding a company will be really, really hard and I still want to do it.		
2	It will be a lengthy process loaded with humiliating failures along the way, and I must learn from them and not take them personally.		
3	I cannot do it alone.		
4	The path to success is not an algorithm with set rules to follow, but an iterative process where I can only increase or decrease the odds of success, but I cannot guarantee anything. Even if I achieve success, it is only temporary.		
5	The goal is to make an "anti-fragile" organization—one that gets stronger over time when faced with problems, failures, uncertainty, and surprises.		
6	When others provide advice, I will listen, but I will also recognize that it is up to me to choose which advice to implement, and how to implement it, since only I own the final results and accountability.		
7	I will have to leave my comfort zone every day to grow and continue to be successful.		
8	I am doing this for more than the money. I believe in my cause and my team.		

[1] Edward B. Roberts, *Entrepreneurs in High Technology: Lessons from MIT and Beyond* (New York: Oxford University Press, 1991), 258.

You may want to consider additional questions customized to your personal situation. The goal is to gauge whether you meet the minimal level of "informed passion" that is required to start a company.

If you did not answer "Yes" to all of these questions, don't start a company today.

And that's okay. I estimate that at least half of my students fall into the category of what I call the "entrepreneurial tourist" or "curious/exploratory entrepreneur." These are people who are interested in learning about how to start a company, but they're not ready to quit their job tomorrow and pour their lives into a fledgling company. Some of my other students are interested in corporate entrepreneurship, or in being an "entrepreneurship amplifier," where they work to increase interest in entrepreneurship and build up resources that will support startups.[2]

All of these people will benefit from going through the 24 Steps with some idea or technology so that they better understand the level of detail that goes into starting a company. And someday if they become ready to start a company, they will have a much stronger set of skills and knowledge ready to use. If you are interested in entrepreneurship, I encourage you to go through *Disciplined Entrepreneurship* and this workbook and iterate on an idea all the way through the process. You'll learn a lot that will benefit you in any capacity where you are doing something new, even inside existing companies.

But if you don't have the requisite passion today, you won't be ready for the short-term and long-term challenges that starting a company will bring you.

Once you have confirmed your level of passion, you are ready to consider your existing ideas or technologies or to determine, based on your interests, strengths, and skills, what ideas or technologies may be interesting starting points for you.

YOUR TEAM

Entrepreneurship is not a solo sport. We've seen time and time again that teams of founders have a greater span of knowledge and skills, and they support each other when the going gets tough.

You may already have a team of founders, or you might be looking for people to join you on your journey. *Disciplined Entrepreneurship* lists some resources that are useful for team building, but how to select a team is a much broader topic than I have space for. In this workbook, start by listing out some key details about your existing team members. That will help you in coming up with ideas to pursue and in determining who else you want to join your team.

---

[2]I discussed different levels of interest in entrepreneurship, and their resulting Personas, as part of my keynote speech to the United States Association for Small Business and Enterprise 2016 Conference. You can view slides from the speech at http://www.slideshare.net/billaulet/past-present-and-future-of-entrepreneurship-education-presentation-at-usasbe-conference-jan-10-2016.

Name	How do we know each other?	Knowledge	Skills	Passions/Interests	Founding Team Potential

A simple way I think about balance, skills, and roles on a team is the 3H model—hacker, hustler, and hipster. While not perfect, it has the benefit of simplicity and raising the issue in a fun and easy to remember way.

1. Who on your team is your lead "hacker"? (Hacker is the one who will make the product.)
2. Who on your team is your lead "hustler"? (Hustler is the business person.)
3. Who on your team is your lead "hipster"? (Hipster is the one concerned with the customer experience and design.)

Note: If you are lacking significant capacity in any one of the 3 H's, then you need to have a plan to fill that gap in the short, medium, and long term.

COMING UP WITH AN IDEA OR A TECHNOLOGY

If you already have an idea or a technology that you want to use as the basis for your company, you may be tempted to skip straight ahead to Step 1, Market Segmentation. However, I encourage you to spend some time to fill out the Idea Mini-Canvas or Technology Mini-Canvas below. You may find that your idea or technology is not as "ready to go" as you thought. Or your teammates may have differing opinions, and a brainstorming session will result in a much better starting point that everyone is passionate about.

If you don't have something to start with, the standard advice is to find a problem that needs to be solved that you are passionate about solving. But what does this mean? Let's drill down and make this advice more actionable.

An excellent starting point for a new venture is a "market pull" where you identify an unfilled yet meaningful need to fix some "customer pain," something for which there exists some group of people who are willing to pay money for a solution. We call it "market pull" because you are being pulled by the customer to satisfy an already-defined general market demand. Coming up with a good market pull is hard—otherwise, everyone would start a company. The most important thing for now is to be open to the ideation process (see below) and come up with ideas that your team thinks are worth pursuing. Step 1, Market Segmentation, is where you will rigorously test your idea against the market.

Another starting point can be a "technology push" based on some new-to-the-world concept that has the potential to create new market opportunities. It could be a hardware breakthrough out of a lab with significant intellectual property around it, as we often have at MIT. Or it could be taking a technology-enabled business model or process to a new market. Think of an Uber-like business model that builds a platform between underutilized assets and disaggregated demand to create more efficient markets—such a business is much more viable when every customer has a smartphone in their pocket. Software as a service or data analytics are other good examples. In this approach, your team has a competitive advantage or early passion about an exciting invention and is searching for a market to apply it to so as to create value and impact.

Often people refer to this approach as "a solution looking for a problem" or the metaphor "a hammer looking for a nail," which is an apt description. It can be challenging to take a technology and find a true customer pain. Some teams get too enamored with the technology, and they don't focus and drill down to understand how to get paying customers. Use "technology push" with caution, and pursue only if the knowledge, skills, and passions of your founding team are more inclined toward starting with a technology, and your team understands that paying customers are more important to a startup than cool technology.

Regardless of whether you choose a market pull or technology push, there is a lot you won't yet know about this general problem: How urgent is the problem? How much will the customer pay for a solution? How many people have this problem? What does the competitive landscape look like?

What will be your competitive advantage that makes you stand apart from all other companies? How profitable a business can be built solving this problem?

You will explore those questions, and many more, throughout the 24 Steps, starting with Step 1, Market Segmentation, where you'll put an idea to the test by doing extensive primary market research to determine whether such a customer pain exists from the idea.

For now, your goal is to come up with *general* ideas where, if you focus and spend sufficient time, your team can produce a product that could be the basis of a scalable business you will be excited about. Use the Idea/Technology Brainstorming Notes table (see page 7) to guide your brainstorming. Then, fill out the appropriate Mini-Canvas (see page 7), and begin the 24 Steps.

There are entire books, courses, conferences and even companies focused on the "ideation" process, so I will not try to comprehensively summarize it here. But I have a few key points related to brainstorming in general based on my secondary research and experience:

1. Brainstorming is best done as a team with diverse perspectives. Without the whole team involved, some members may feel less invested in your success. Without diverse perspectives, your ideas may not be broad enough to find a truly great market opportunity.

2. Use improv (improvisation) training techniques with your team. They're effective at getting people to think in the kind of "yes, and…" mindset that fosters effective brainstorming. In "yes, and…" you don't immediately scrutinize and criticize each idea that comes up, but instead you build on each other's ideas. Only after you've come up with a lot of ideas do you start a critical analysis.

3. Brainstorming and the subsequent filtering of ideas is also an excellent way to determine who should be and shouldn't be part of your founding team. While not the expressed purpose of this exercise, this is every bit as valuable, if not more valuable, than coming up with the idea. Since the real work of the new venture has not yet started in any meaningful way, I find this process is more useful in determining who you don't want to work with as opposed to measuring the strength of the founding team.

4. Take brainstorming seriously, but understand this is a small part of the overall process. An idea is necessary to start with, and it gets your team in the right general neighborhood. But I often refer to the initial idea as the single most overrated thing in entrepreneurship. The quality of your team, having a clear target market, and having a sound process for execution (like the 24 Steps) are much more important factors in ultimate success than your initial idea, which often changes dramatically over time.

THE ENTREPRENEURSHIP SUCCESS PIE

Idea/Technology Brainstorming Notes

Use this chart to help identify your team's knowledge, skills, and interests, which can help you come up with market pull (or tech push) ideas.

Knowledge: What was the focus of your education/career?	
Capabilities: What are you most proficient at?	
Connections: Who do you know with expertise in different industries? Do you know other entrepreneurs?	
Financial assets: Do you have access to significant financial capital, or will you be relying on personal savings to start?	
Past work/life experience: In previous jobs you've held, or in previous experiences in your life, what inefficiencies or "pain points" existed?	
Passion for a particular market: Do you want to improve healthcare? Education? Energy? Transportation?	

Market Pull Mini-Canvas

1. WHAT:	**2. URGENCY:**
What is the general problem we are trying to solve or the opportunity we are looking to capitalize on? _____ _____ _____ _____	This is a: (circle one) • Vitamin pill (i.e., nice to have) • Pain killer (i.e., solves a critical problem) • Game changer (i.e., opens new market opportunities)
3. WHY US:	**4. PASSION:**
Our team has or would have the following assets that would make us uniquely qualified to implement this idea: _____ _____ _____ _____	Summarize why our team cares so much about this idea that we are willing to embark on this arduous & humbling journey: _____ _____ _____ _____ _____

Technology Push Mini-Canvas

1. WHAT:	**2. WHY US:**
Description of the invention/technology: _____ _____ _____ _____ _____	Why we have a significant advantage over anyone else with regard to this invention: _____ _____ _____ _____
3. LEAP FORWARD:	**4. PASSION:**
Compared with the most relevant current alternative, why is it so compelling that it will make people and industries change: _____ _____ _____ _____ _____	Summarize why our team cares so much about this idea that we are willing to embark on this arduous and humbling journey: _____ _____ _____ _____ _____

HYBRID IDEA: MIX OF MARKET PULL AND TECHNOLOGY PUSH

When I wrote *Disciplined Entrepreneurship*, I sought simplicity as much as possible, so I divided starting points neatly into idea or technology. But as the mathematician Alfred North Whitehead said, "Seek simplicity and distrust it." Now, after seeing hundreds of companies applying the 24 Steps, I trust it more, but I have also found areas that deserve greater explanation, and this is one such area.

The reality is that most often teams start with market pull, but there is some technology push, especially from universities and research and development laboratories. In some cases, however, teams start somewhere in between the two models of market pull or technology push. Over the past few years I have seen increased awareness of market importance at all levels. Today, even the scientist in the lab is thinking early on about the application of the breakthrough he or she is working on. Something that seems like a "technology push" may have been inspired by a "market pull," and vice versa.

An example of a hybrid idea came from one of my students, Parul Singh, who began with the fundamental concepts that teachers need help, and new technology like the iPad enabled exciting opportunities to do so. The convergence of the demand and the sudden ubiquity of tablets was an opportunity for her to create a company she was extremely excited about. While things changed over time, this hybrid idea was sufficiently compelling to get her and her cofounder, Dante Cassanego, to start the journey toward creating Gradeable, which had the goal of reimagining how grade-school students are assessed in order to increase student engagement in the classroom.

So if your originating concept is a hybrid, which will be true in many cases, you should use both Mini-Canvases, but I would more strongly emphasize the market pull one. Then I would suggest you overlay these Mini-Canvases with the following Hybrid Mini-Canvas.

Hybrid Idea Consolidated Mini-Canvas

I. MARKET PULL:	2. TECHNOLOGY PUSH:
This idea is relevant to the _____ _____ market because it will produce significant value by _____ _____ _____ _____ _____ _____	The enabling technology invention is: _____ _____ _____ _____ _____ _____ _____

3. WHY US:
What makes us especially qualified to pursue this opportunity?
_____
_____
_____
_____

Your analysis of the customer and the marketplace will lead your journey through the 24 Steps, not your idea or technology, no matter how amazing you think it is now. This step is just the starting point of a long journey. Let's move on. Onward and upward!

STEP 1

Market Segmentation

WHAT IS STEP 1, MARKET SEGMENTATION?

Brainstorm how your idea or technology can serve a variety of potential end users. Narrow that list of potential end users to several promising categories, then conduct primary market research to gain more information about each potential end user.

WHY DO WE DO THIS STEP, AND WHY DO WE DO IT NOW?

It is crucial to start the process with a focus on a target customer. Everything else about your business will be based on that focus.

> **By the Book:** See pages 23–35 of *Disciplined Entrepreneurship* for basic knowledge on this step.
> See pages 36–39 of *Disciplined Entrepreneurship* for an example of how a company addressed this step.

 vs.

Seeing the world through the eyes of the customer vs. Seeing the world through the perspective of the company

The Market Segmentation step gives you the right frame of mind for the new product right from the start.

PROCESS GUIDE

The single necessary and sufficient condition for a business is a paying customer. If people don't give you money in exchange for your product, nothing else matters. As I discuss in *Disciplined Entrepreneurship*, the best way for an innovative startup to lay the groundwork for a solid company is to dominate a narrow, carefully defined market that serves a particular end user. To choose the best market, you'll do a Market Segmentation that uses primary market research to pinpoint the best markets to draw your attention. Later, you'll select one of these markets and dig deeper in the process of determining exactly who your customer will be.

An end user (the foundation of a market segment) is a category of people who have similar needs and customer pains. End users typically have similar demographics and other characteristics. Rigorously categorizing end users, which is what you want to do, is much more detailed than you may think. For instance, an education startup would be poorly served by targeting the general category "teachers" as their end users, as it is too general. This general description ignores the differences between public and private schools; primary, secondary, and postsecondary education; rural, suburban, and urban school districts; and young, inexperienced teachers and older, veteran teachers.

In this workbook, you'll go through the three stages of Market Segmentation—brainstorming, narrowing, and primary market research.

Part 1A: Brainstorming

"I already have my idea. Why do I need to brainstorm again?"

The idea or technology is a good starting point because it reveals your interests, skills, passions, and possibly key assets. But it often does not articulate systematically enough a customer pain, a need that is so deep that a group of people are willing to pay you a meaningful amount of money to solve it. The Market Segmentation's brainstorming stage is designed to broaden the world of possible end users as wide as possible to consider who might benefit from your idea.

Often some of the most interesting Beachhead Markets exist on the fringe of the spectrum and are overlooked by others, so think broadly. Wild ideas are welcome and encouraged at this point.

How do you effectively brainstorm so that you are considering all the possibilities? Keep these tips in mind:

1. **Get the right people in the conversation:** You should discuss with not just your founders, but also consider other relevant parties such as domain experts, technologists, creative types, facilitators, and others you deem appropriate. It is helpful to have many of these people in a room together brainstorming, but don't expect to lock yourselves in a room for a single session of a few hours and have a completed list; you also want to bounce ideas off of potential customers and others you know or can get connected to. To get the best portfolio of options, it will probably take multiple meetings in multiple different locations with multiple different audiences within the time frame you have available for your situation. Don't let the discussion be constrained by the technology available today. If anything, expand your horizons and consider trends in technology and even brainstorm the possibilities if technology advanced even faster.

2. **Be clear on the dual purpose of the brainstorming:** You want to get the right people in the conversation because you're not just making a comprehensive list of potential markets. You're also selecting and refining your initial team and then creating alignment for that foundational team. Some of the people you invite to the conversation will become cofounders, and depending on how the conversation goes, some of your current cofounders may drop out. This is natural and healthy if you are executing the process effectively. Cohesion comes from all the members of the team participating in the formation of your organization and understanding its direction. Just knowing the final answer is not as empowering as deeply understanding why the answer was agreed upon.

3. **Get in the right place with the right tools:** Find a new place where everyone feels comfortable because it is important that constraining hierarchical relationships and distractions are eliminated or at least kept to a minimum. Disconnect from all e-mails, texts, tweets, and other notifications for at least a half day—a full day is better. Get a lot of sticky notes and encourage participants to jot down ideas as they come up with them and then share them. If you can find a space with whiteboard or chalkboard walls, even better.

4. **Get the right rules to brainstorm by:** The renowned design firm IDEO has five basic rules that govern brainstorming sessions. While others have used variants of this and customized them to their environment (quite colorfully and memorably), IDEO's rules that can be used as a starting point are:

   a. Defer judgment

   b. One conversation at a time

   c. Stay focused on the topic

   d. Encourage wild ideas

   e. Build on the ideas of others

5. **Identify, empower, and develop a facilitator:** Find or appoint a facilitator to enforce the rules you agree to in #4 above, and empower that person to guide the process. That person should take this responsibility seriously and prepare for the session. It is their responsibility to ensure everyone gets input and to avoid groupthink or dominant personalities controlling the conversation.

6. **Get everyone in the right mood:** As discussed in Step 0 of this workbook, getting people in the mindset of "yes, and…" is incredibly important. The night before the brainstorming session, I strongly suggest having participants watch the brainstorming part (approximately the first third) of ABC News *Nightline's* segment "The Deep Dive" about IDEO; you can find this video online. On the day of the brainstorming session, start out with David Morris's 11-minute TEDxVictoria talk on "The Way of Improv," also available online. The participants will hopefully be laughing by now and more relaxed than usual. The facilitator should then explain the key points of the David Morris video and how that builds off the IDEO video and is relevant to the exercise of the day. The fundamental concept of saying "yes, and…" has helped so many of my interactions with students and entrepreneurs to make situations much more productive.

7. **Focus on being specific:** The "F" word for entrepreneurs is "focus," because it's hard to do, and entrepreneurship requires continually keeping your focus. Make sure everyone understands they are brainstorming potential end users, and have them review Step 1 of *Disciplined*

Entrepreneurship, which provides examples about how narrowly end users should be defined. Do not worry now about who will pay for the product; focus instead on end users who would gain significant value from some permutation of your idea. If there is no end user, there will be no economic buyer.

8. **First pass to get the ideas out:** Don't critique, combine, reject, or otherwise discourage ideas. Just get them out and write them down in a nonjudgmental fashion.

The worksheet below is almost a blank slate, and that's because the brainstorming process should be free flowing. Use the worksheet as a loose guide but let your imagination flow.

Brainstorming What My Startup Will Do

What is my idea or technology?		
What industries and end users could my idea or technology apply to?		
Industry or Similar Category	End Users	What They Would Use It For

Part 1B: Narrow

Now that you have lots of ideas, it is time to start narrowing down the field to eliminate from consideration market segments that would be weak options for your startup. The goal is to get to a manageable list so that later you can do a deeper analysis on a small number of market segments before you choose your Beachhead Market. I would say anywhere from four to 10 markets is a reasonable number of candidates to end up with, so that you can build your first draft Market Segmentation Matrix in Part 1C of this step.

Use the seven questions in the chart below as a guide for your discussions. Refer to Step 1 in *Disciplined Entrepreneurship* if you need more detail on how to answer those questions.

Start by focusing on your team's values, passions, and goals, and eliminate ideas that violate your values. Don't ignore your passions, because you will not be successful if you do something you do not like. You will probably also have some subset of ideas that the team quickly decides are not worth pursuing.

Each time, before you eliminate a market segment, allow time for the group to discuss to make sure the group has all the information before making such a decision. This discussion can be a powerful learning and alignment process. Lastly, once the obvious candidates are removed, have the group vote on the remaining market segments to get a prioritized list.

Use the chart below to record your prioritized list of top market segments and why they are particularly compelling. Record a sentence or two explaining each question on the chart. If, while filling out this chart, your team realizes another market segment is more compelling, discuss with the group whether to switch it out on your short list of candidates. Then, use the "Rank" column to prioritize each end user by how compelling an opportunity you think it is ("1" is best).

Top Target Markets to Consider for My Startup

End user	Target customer well-funded?	Target customer readily accessible to sales force?	Target customer's compelling reason to buy?	Can you deliver a whole product?	Is there entrenched competition?	Can you leverage this segment to enter others?	Consistent with values, passions, goals of team?	Rank

Part 1C: Primary Market Research and Market Segmentation Matrix Version 1.0

Now that you have narrowed your market segments to a manageable number, you will start doing primary market research to build out the Market Segmentation Matrix below. You may be tempted to fill in the matrix with what you already know, but I urge you to be patient.

Instead, gather nearly all of the information through primary market research, by interacting directly with potential customers how they work today and what their customer pains are. Don't assume you have the answer for a customer and start advocating your ideas. Instead, stay firmly in "inquiry mode" and learn from the customer. You will discover lots of things you don't know about the customer's needs, and you may find reason to revise your end user market segment definitions.

Before starting your primary market research, each person working on the matrix should read and understand the next chapter in this workbook, "A Practical Guide to Primary Market Research," and should sign its "Primary Market Research Pledge." Getting unbiased market feedback through observations, interviews, and experiments is absolutely crucial to your success.

Do not allow anyone to get too fixed in their opinion early in the process (i.e., stubborn). It is very easy to come to a strong point of view and then start advocating for it too early in the process. If someone appears to be leaning in that direction, the facilitator or someone in the group should openly note it and ask that person to explain the counterarguments to their own proposal, to get them thinking more broadly about both the pros and cons. It is important that people not be driving stakes in the ground with regard to their position, since it will make it emotionally hard for them to change later. You don't have sufficient data at this point to make decisions; you need to do your primary market research.

The best way to tackle the matrix is to assign each market segment to a subgroup within the team—hopefully more than one person so that the resulting analysis benefits from multiple perspectives. Set a deadline to get a first pass done on the matrix. Each team should talk to and/or closely observe a minimum of 10 potential end users from that market segment during the first pass.

After the first pass is complete, have the team come back together and discuss their findings, so that the group can give feedback on each market segment. A few markets may now be eliminated, and the remaining market segments can get even more attention in a second round of primary market research. Do not allow individual personalities or debating skills to dictate which market is chosen, but rather a systematic analysis. Passion does matter, but it needs to be the passion of the group, coupled with a rigorous and realistic analysis.

As we mentioned earlier in this section, it is important that when discussing the first pass results, if anyone seems to be getting too emotionally attached to a market, ask them to argue why the team should not pursue that market. If they still appear to be too attached, swap individuals and allow someone else to continue the research of that market segment.

You will want to iterate multiple times on your matrix, alternating back and forth between primary market research and group discussion of your findings. Getting the matrix as correct as possible will make it easier to achieve forward momentum and save you lots of time later. But institute deadlines for each iteration of the matrix to keep things moving forward at an acceptable pace. Forward progress is essential.

Once you have obtained consensus within the team that you have the best Market Segmentation Matrix you can build in the time frame that is acceptable to your situation, you are ready to move on to the next step in the 24 Steps. Participants should be aware they cannot expect to pull you back to restart this process unless there is truly overwhelming evidence agreed by all that the current market segment selection is not viable. You need to move forward with everyone in agreement. While it is possible that in a later step of the 24 Steps you will get some significant new information that was impossible to know previously, forcing you to revisit the Market Segmentation, in general iterating all the way back to the beginning is the most expensive kind of iteration because all of your work builds off each previous step. Completing the matrix puts your team at a "speak now or forever hold your peace" moment.

Market Segmentation Matrix Row Definitions

1	Market Segment Name	Carefully name the market segment so it appropriately and precisely captures the group you want and no more; it is okay to be general at first, but you will have to narrow this down in time to make real progress.
2	End User	This is the person who is actually using the product, not the economic buyer or the champion (more on this in Step 12)—even if you are selling to a company or a general organization, you want to list here the people in that company who will be using your product.
3	Task	What exactly is it that the end users do that you will significantly affect or allow them to do that they could not do before?
4	Benefit	What is the benefit that you believe the end users will get?
5	Urgency of Need	What is the level of urgency to solve the problem or capture the new opportunity for the end user?
6	Example End Users	Who are examples of end users that you can, have, or will talk to, so as to validate your perceptions of this market segment?
7	Lead Customers	Who are the influential customers (i.e., lighthouse customers) where, if they buy the product, others will take note and likely follow?
9	Willingness to Change	How conservative is this market segment? How open are they to change? Is there something to force change (e.g., impending crisis)?
10	Frequency of Buying	How often do they buy new products? What does their buying cycle look like at a high level?
11	Concentration of Buyers	How many different buyers are there in this market segment? Is it a monopoly? Oligopoly (a small number of buyers)? Or many competitive buyers?
12	Other Relevant Market Considerations	This allows for customization of your segment for relevant considerations such as "high employee turnover," "very low margins/commodity," "high-growth industry," "high virality effect" (i.e., word of mouth), etc.
13	Size of Market (# of End Users)	Estimation of the number of end users to a relevant range (10s, 100s, 1Ks, 10Ks, 100Ks, 1Ms, etc.).
14	Est. Value of End User ($1, $10, $100, $1K, etc.)	A first-pass estimate of the value of each end user, again to a relevant order of magnitude so you can make some relative decisions now (you will do a deep dive into this and other numbers later).
15	Competition/ Alternatives	What will be your competition from the end users' perspective? Include the "do nothing" option as well as who else would be competitors if the end users analyzed their options.
16	Other Components Needed for a Full Solution	Since most customers will only buy a full solution and not an individual component that they have to assemble into a full solution, what other elements are needed to construct a full solution to achieve the benefits above? These are the complementary assets that you do not currently have but would need to build or acquire to give the end user a full solution.
17	Important Partners	Who are the partners or distributors you will have to work with to fit into the end user's workflow (e.g., data must come out of vendor A's system and then be picked up at the end by vendor B's system) or business processes (e.g., the end user gets all his or her product via distribution channel C)?
18	Other Relevant Personal Considerations	In many Market Segmentation analyses, there are additional important factors that should be considered. These could be things like where the market segment is geographically centered, whether it matches the values of the founding team, existing knowledge and contacts in market, etc.

Market Segmentation Matrix Starter Template

Market Segment Name					
End User					
Task					
Benefit					
Urgency of Need					
Example End Users					
Lead Customers					
Willingness to Change					
Frequency of Buying					
Concentration of Buyers					
Other Relevant Market Segment Considerations					
Size of Market (# of End Users)					
Est. Value of End User ($1, $10, $100, $1K, etc.)					
Competition/Alternatives					
Other Components Needed for a Full Solution					
Important Partners					
Other Relevant Personal Considerations					

Team Composition and Dynamics

Before you move on to Step 2, Select a Beachhead Market, consider the team you have assembled. Throughout this step, you should have been keeping an eye on the team composition and dynamics. Be open and honest about how things are working and if everyone should continue with the project. It will be much easier to change team members now than later.

You know it is crucial to iterate on your product to be successful, but your team's composition and cohesion is just as important, if not more important. And yet, people are reluctant to iterate on their team. Don't be like that. You all will pay later if you don't optimize your team now.

I've included the following team table from Step 0. Consider it again, including not just the founders you initially identified, but other participants in the brainstorming process of this step. Which of them may have valuable insights, perspectives, and experiences? If they do not want to join the team, are there others with similar qualities you want to add? Are there members who you do not think would contribute positively to the team?

Name	How Do We Know Each Other?	Knowledge	Skills	Passions/Interests	Founding Team Potential

Make sure you document your decisions so everyone has a clear understanding of how you are going forward, and so team members understand their "ownership" of the business venture. Even if you are not quite ready to incorporate your business, you don't want a misunderstanding at this early stage to fester and cause trouble for your team later on. Getting legal help may be a wise strategy at this point. The 24 Steps do not cover legal issues related to company formation, such as how to split equity between team members, but Noam Wasserman's *The Founder's Dilemmas* is a good initial resource to better understand how to manage team dynamics in a startup.

BONUS TOPIC

―――――

A Practical Guide to Primary Market Research

―――――

This is new material that was only covered at a high level in *Disciplined Entrepreneurship*. I want to express my thanks to my colleague Elaine Chen at the Martin Trust Center for MIT Entrepreneurship, as well as the entire marketing group at the MIT Sloan School of Management, specifically Professors Catherine Tucker, Duncan Simester, and Drazen Prelec, who provided important intellectual contributions and consultations with regard to this chapter. The good ideas are theirs, and I take full responsibility for interpretations or extrapolations to the entrepreneurial environment that might be more controversial.

―――――

WHAT IS PRIMARY MARKET RESEARCH?

Primary market research is direct interaction with customers to understand their situation. The skills required to do effective primary market research are required to complete almost every step of the 24 Steps. Step 1, Market Segmentation, is heavily fueled by primary market research, but you never stop doing primary market research when you want paying customers.

I've added this supplemental material to help you develop a fundamental skill that underlies the entire process of starting a company—the knowledge and ability to do good primary market research. *Disciplined Entrepreneurship* gives an overview of the topic, but this chapter will help you research much more efficiently and effectively.

The entrepreneurship community has lagged behind in incorporating primary market research into startup formation, which is a missed opportunity. Customer-focused companies such as Procter and Gamble and leading product design firms such as IDEO and Continuum Innovation have long practiced primary market research in their user-centered design processes.

More recently, with terms like Steve Blank's "customer discovery," primary market research is becoming less intimidating an idea for entrepreneurs. But primary market research has deep roots, and this chapter explores the depth and breadth of academic and practitioner insights on the topic.

*Primary market research feeds into the 24 Steps all along the way and is the
fuel that keeps the process going in the right direction.*

Entire books have been written on this topic, so I am going to try to synthesize it down to what entrepreneurs really need to know to be successful. As Dharmesh Shah says, one of the key things you need to do to be successful in a startup is to start. It is right there in the name. So don't get over-whelmed by the magnitude of this task; just get started.

Definitions

- **Primary Market Research:** When you (or someone you hire) directly interact with the potential customer to gain knowledge specific to your potential new venture. I will often call this "bottom-up" market information. Depending on where you are in the 24 Steps, you may be interacting with the end user or with other individuals within the company, such as the people who make spending decisions (the "economic buyers"), the people who will advocate for the purchase of your product (the "champions"), or others who influence or control the procurement process (collectively, the entire group is called the "Decision-Making Unit," which I will get into much more detail in Step 12).

- **Secondary Research:** Material you get from sources other than the potential customer. It is indirect. It is generally not specific to your business. These are the industry and government reports that you can find on the Internet or buy from a source that has already done them. I will refer to this as "top-down" market information.

- **Qualitative vs. Quantitative Research:** Qualitative research is exploratory research that helps you generally understand a topic, and is often conducted through a small number of open-ended in-person interviews. Quantitative research uses a much more structured approach and focuses on gathering specific data to prove or disprove the hypotheses created in the qualitative phase.

- **Ethnographic Research:** Technically defined as the systematic study of people and cultures. In primary market research, it turns out that customer psyche plays an important role in decision making. Sometimes, it is even more important than a rational or economic perspective. However, you can't ask people directly why they do what they do, because people are bad at explaining their habits. And yet it is essential for you to understand this behavior. Anthropologists have been doing ethnographic research for a long time. They embed themselves in the cultures they are studying and observe closely to gain this information.

The Goal of Primary Market Research

The goal of good primary market research is to understand your customer in all dimensions: rationally, emotionally, economically, socially, culturally, and more. Not only have you walked a mile in your customer's shoes, but you understand them better than they understand themselves. Good primary market research is not just numbers, and it does not start with numbers, but rather that holistic understanding of the customer—the person. Only then can you solve significant problems or otherwise motivate and provide value to the customer.

It is not the customer's job to design your new product. That is your job. As Elaine Chen says, "The customer is the expert of their problem, and you are the expert in finding a solution to that problem." It is your responsibility to systematically get enough unbiased information to design and then refine a new product that will create significant value for the customer, and many others just like him or her.

Good primary market research is a continuous process of generating new insights and then converting them into testable hypotheses. You will then continue to use primary market research to validate or invalidate these hypotheses. You may go through the 24 Steps to launch your product based off primary market research, but in reality, the process never ends. Customers and markets change over time, so what is true one year may be invalid the next. Primary market research is an essential skill set for a great entrepreneurial team to have, and it makes being an entrepreneur a lot more fun, too.

The Five Biggest Obstacles to Good Primary Market Research

The fundamental concept of primary market research is quite simple—go out and observe, listen, and interact with potential customers. That can be very hard for some people (i.e., engineers) and very easy for others. Even if it sounds easy, it is not. Here are some of the pitfalls that you have to be aware of before you start.

1. **Lack of Structured Process:** While there needs to be flexibility in how you obtain information, you have to have a process and know the process—and know that it is a process! I will step you through that process here, and there are many other resources available to you that I will reference at the end of this chapter.

2. **Not Properly Executing the Designed Process:** No process will work if it is not used, and this is no exception. You cannot come up with the right answers without interacting with others. You must get out and talk, observe, and test hypotheses with real potential customers, which often results in answers you would not have gotten on your own. You must dig and get good initial sources to talk to and then grow your sources. You have to learn the process and execute it with good technique. Good technique has a lot to do with avoiding the biases I cover in the next three points.

3. **Confirmation Bias:** Extremely common for all people during research, confirmation bias is when you only see the information that confirms your worldview. You ignore or block out

any information that runs counter to your hypothesis. A good way to counter this tendency is to set up criteria beforehand that will confirm or disprove your hypothesis so that you don't change the metrics for success once you start. Even then, bias can still creep in based on how you structure your questions and surveys, inadvertently prompting the customer to provide the answers you want to hear. You must be neutral and not "lead the witness."

4. **Selection Bias:** The people you interview, whether during qualitative or quantitative research, may not be a good representation of the opinions of the group as a whole. Think about Internet polls that allow everyone to vote without controlling for demographics. The type of people who vote do so in percentages that far exceed their true representation of the broader population. As such they produce wildly inaccurate projections. This is why political candidates like U.S. presidential aspirant Ron Paul, with a very passionate base, have done so well on Internet polls, despite not gaining traction in general elections. You need to really understand what your sample should look like to produce meaningful results and control for variations between people that will affect your results. Sometimes, selection bias can be exacerbated by not clearly defining who your customer is. If your end user is "women" and you are at the mall interviewing or observing potential end users, will a 15-year-old affluent urban female have similar opinions as a 40-year-old middle-class suburban mother of three kids? Think about whether your definition of end user is too broad to achieve reliable research results.[1]

5. **Social Acceptability Bias:** If you engage with family or friends, they will most likely not give you accurate answers because they don't want to offend you by not liking your ideas. They will be polite rather than brutally honest because they want to keep their social relationship strong. You need brutally honest feedback from unbiased people, so it is best to interact with people who do not have a social connection with you. Similarly, on sensitive topics like race or sexuality, you may have trouble getting honest answers, particularly with in-person or phone interviews as compared to anonymous surveys.

There are other biases such as the IKEA effect (once you build a product, your confirmation bias gets much stronger), giving the more entertaining interview more weight, giving the last interview more consideration, etc. It is good to realize your biases and always be on the lookout for them. Being data-driven is good, but the data can be made to mislead as well, so that is not a sufficient answer. A great way to minimize biases is to have multiple people conducting the research who have been trained on the biases inherent in research, so that multiple perspectives will keep things honest.

Process and Techniques

This is the streamlined process I have used and encouraged others to use. It is not as comprehensive as those used in big companies, especially those market research powerhouses like Procter and Gamble, but you don't have the resources or time to be able to do it that way. You have to get the biggest bang for the buck, so this is an efficient, simplified process guide.

---

[1] As Elaine Chen points out, selection bias is especially pernicious in qualitative research because it is by nature anecdotal with low sample points. Imagine talking to five people who seem to validate your hypothesis and you stop there, and it turns out that there exists nobody else on Earth who agrees with them. You have a lot less of this problem when running a survey with 500 people who respond, assuming you have randomly chosen who within the larger group you survey, and you controlled for the right variables by incorporating demographic or other questions into the survey and weighting the responses.

1. **Make a Plan:** Many of you will do what I did the first time I learned about primary market research, which was just going out and start talking to potential customers without a plan. This is not disciplined. Develop a plan. This may sound obvious, but it was not to me at first, and it may not be to you. Without a plan, your potential customers will get frustrated after they talk to you once when you come back with more questions that could have been addressed up front. This customer, a very valuable and precious source of information, will then write you off as disorganized and wasting their time. Please save yourself a lot of suffering and losing some potential great sources by having a thoughtful plan.

   A general plan will look much like the following from Elaine Chen's Primary Market Research Primer Guide[2]:

   1. Write out the goals and objectives of the research, and a detailed description of the research technique.

   2. Define recruitment criteria for interviewees.

   3. Develop a recruitment questionnaire.

   4. Develop supporting content (e.g., discussion guide, landing page, online survey).

   5. Recruit subjects.

   6. Run the research program.

   7. Digest results, next steps.

   Of these items, the supporting content is often the most overlooked for its value, particularly the discussion guide. In any in-person or phone interview, a discussion guide is crucial so that you know the key questions you should ask each person, in part for consistency but also to make sure each interview yields all the information you need. It will allow you to have a structured dialogue with the person you are engaging with while maintaining flexibility. Likely, you will constantly update this discussion guide at the beginning, but once you have done sufficient interviews, the changes become much less frequent.

2. **Start with Secondary Research . . . But Not Too Much:** Before you go out and start to do primary market research, do some homework so you know at least the basics of the industry. Don't do so much that you think you are an expert of any kind, but don't be totally naïve. You will be wasting the time of those you engage with if you don't know the basics. On the other hand, don't assume all your secondary research is accurate, because sometimes the most interesting opportunities are where conventional wisdom hasn't kept up with, or never matched at all, the reality in the marketplace.

3. **Start Qualitative Before Quantitative:** The most common mistake is to start with a survey. You have to figure out the right questions to ask in a survey, so surveys are useful later but not up front. And while you'll start by asking specific questions to make sure their demographic (age, gender, etc.) and psychographic (personality, opinions, lifestyles) characteristics match your target customer group, your research questions should be very open-ended, such as, "Please describe a good day for you. Now describe a bad day." Another question that some experienced primary market research experts prefer is, "Tell me about the last time you did X." Always follow up with, "Why?," "Why not?," or "You said X. Can you say more?" Get them to tell you real specific

---

[2]Elaine Chen's Primary Market Research Primer presentation can be found at http://www.slideshare.net/chenelaine/primary-market-research-an-overview-on-qualitative-and-quantitative-research-techniques.

examples. These examples or stories are generally very powerful and easy for the customer to tell you about. Don't add friction by asking for data or too many facts right now. You are probing for those big pain points, the biggest fears and motivators, in their lives. While your interview will be loosely scripted, let the customer take the conversation wherever they want it to go.

4. **Source Candidates to Engage With, and Use Them to Find More Candidates:** The best places to find candidates are at the "watering holes" for your target customer. Watering holes are those places where your target customer congregates physically or digitally. For many religions, that is their place of worship. For fitness enthusiasts, it is probably their high-end gym. For women about to get married, it is Pinterest. For others, it might well be an industry group or conference. For baby-boomer health-conscious consumers, it might well be Whole Foods. Find out what the watering holes are for your target customer because that will be a highly efficient place to begin engaging them. The sourcing process requires some creativity, as do all the parts of the process, but here are some ideas to help you source leads and make initial contact:

   a. **Physical watering holes:** While digital watering holes can be convenient, you need to be comfortable physically getting out of your workplace and interact directly with your target customer.

   b. **LinkedIn or Facebook groups:** You can usually find a group that is tied to your target customer and may even be arranged around the problem you are looking to solve. Today this is most often LinkedIn and Facebook, but for your target customer it might be Instagram, Snapchat, or Twitter. This will also change over time as new virtual discussion forums become popular and the existing ones fall out of favor.

   c. **Blogs or online discussions:** Similar to LinkedIn/Facebook groups. These digital meeting places are very efficient ways of finding candidates, but respect the rules of the blog or forum or you might get banned from the website.

   d. **Industry groups and membership lists:** A form of watering hole. Depending on the list, you may get a lower response rate than with some of the above methods.

   e. **Ads:** You can advertise on Google or Facebook, targeted at specific demographics, for as little as $20 to get the names of interested people and then follow up. And if no one responds, that's important information as well. To be most effective, you should carefully craft the wording of your ads, or you may spend a lot of money getting a lot of responses from people who are not truly in your target customer group.

   f. **Read Publicly Available Information:** When you do your secondary research, you will likely run across some names linked to your market. Write those names down and find contact information for them. There are various tools to help you find someone's e-mail address (one I know of is emailhunter.co, but there are many others as well). When you contact them, you should be ready for rejection or, more likely, no response, but it only takes one to respond and then you are in. Like the camel's nose in the tent, you can expand from there. You may also want to try engaging with key people on social media like Twitter and build up a relationship that way.

   g. **The Last Question:** Once you get going, the best way to get candidates is from others in the target customer group. As such, your last question at the end of each interview should be, "Who else do you know that has a similar challenge or opportunity to you that I should speak to? Would you be willing to make an introduction?" Once you find one lead, your goal is to have your list grow by getting multiple new leads from every interview.

5. **Initial Contact:** Now that you have your initial list of people to contact (a list that should continually be growing as you do your research), things get real. You have to persuade your contact to give you at least 15 minutes of their time, depending on how many questions you have, and that is not easy if you are working with a "cold lead" where you are making first contact. When you initially contact the candidate, it is good to reference someone they know. That is easier than ever with LinkedIn, which shows you mutual connections for each person you look up. Start with short e-mails or dialogue to build credibility and rapport. Explain that you are doing research on their industry to try to help make it better, including their job. Be *completely* in inquiry mode and not one bit in sales or advocacy mode at this point. You are not really a company yet, nor do you have a product. If you think you are a company, then that is a problem. Be empathetic to making their job better, because that will show in your interactions. Still, be steeled for lots of rejection. There is copious research about little tips and techniques for interacting with cold leads. For instance, Tina Seelig at Stanford found that if you are physically approaching strangers, it is better to have a female than a male make the interaction.[3] At first, you will probably feel as if making these initial contacts will never work, but you have to stay at it and then it will get much better. It is never easy, but it gets much easier the more you do it.

6. **Act Like a Great Journalist:** I have not been a journalist but have been so impressed when I have interacted with and observed great journalists in action. They have great active listening techniques to get people to talk. The great ones listen with 150 percent of their attention. They have a positive voice and physical stance when engaging. They are incredibly interested and empathetic. They shake their head and say "yes" a lot and are nonjudgmental. They lean forward and listen intently, and visibly so. They make the person being interviewed feel like the most important person in the world. Oh yes, and make sure to smile and be enthusiastic. Humor can help, but sarcasm is not good. The person must like you before they will open up. A couple of ways to verbally engage are using the person's name a lot and repeating back to the person the words they've said.

7. **If You Can, Have Two People Conduct the Interview:** Having two people conduct the interview allows one person to concentrate completely on engaging the interviewee while the others is taking detailed notes and observing the interviewee's nonverbal signals from another angle. Make sure to write down not just what the person says, but the nonverbal reactions as well. Having two people in the room also allows you more perspectives when reviewing notes afterward.

8. **Constantly Make Sure You Are Interviewing the Right People:** If you interview people who are not in your target customer group, you will get spurious information that will not help you understand your target customer, and in fact may confuse you or lead you astray. Make sure you put together a short recruitment questionnaire (it doesn't have to be longer than five questions) as part of your research plan that screens out people not in your target customer group. This helps you avoid the aforementioned and ever-present selection bias.

9. **As You Get to Forming Hypotheses, Small "n" Might Well Be Better Than Big "n":** After you have done some qualitative research, you will begin to form hypotheses about ways you might be able to benefit the target customer. But you don't want to spend forever on qualitative research to test it out, because you don't have the time. MIT Professor Drazen Prelec expresses it as small "n" (number of candidates) and big "n," where small "n" is a small enough

---

[3]Seelig, Tina, *What I Wish I Knew When I Was 20*, Chapter 1, HarperOne, 2009.

group size that you can go deep in each interview to understand what is causing the phenomenon you feel is important. A bigger "n" gives you more candidates but less in-depth understanding. In the qualitative stage the smaller "n" is better; then, in the quantitative stage, the larger "n" becomes more relevant to test it out more broadly once you understand the hypothesis in a robust manner.

10. **You Should Be Surprised:** As Catherine Tucker points out, the goal of qualitative primary market research is to develop new hypotheses; so if you are not surprised, you are probably not learning anything. That defeats the purpose of the process. It would also be a pretty clear sign of confirmation bias if you never learn anything, and that is not a positive thing.

11. **Moving to Quantitative:** Once you have developed credible hypotheses for the small "n" sample through your qualitative methods, then you should start to test them more systematically. The scripts and the surveys now get more structured, and you are looking at scripts and surveys that will start to produce numbers, points on a cluster map, and the like. You will now get the data to validate, invalidate, somewhat validate, somewhat invalidate, or leave in the TBD column for your hypotheses.

12. **Perceived as Opposed to Real Value:** Often, as MIT Sloan marketing Professor Duncan Simester has shown in his research, there is a gap between real and perceived value. Both matter, as does the gap. In both your qualitative and quantitative research, understand the difference. Look to understand each of these and then quantify at the end as much as possible.

13. **Don't Always Believe What Is Said:** Often people say things with the best of intent but then do different things in reality. What they do matters more than what they say. A/B testing, where customers are randomly divided into groups and are treated differently to see how the difference in treatment affects the customer's response. Likewise, and well-designed behavioral economics experiments are good ways to see what customers will really do regardless of what they say. You will explore this topic in more detail in Step 21, Test Key Assumptions.

Results

How do you know when primary market research is complete? It never is. Entrepreneurs and good businesspeople are constantly talking with customers and seeing new opportunities and refining their offerings. That said, there are times when you have enough primary market research to continue to the next step in the 24 Steps. You'll generally know you are at this point when your hypotheses are being validated and new customer contacts are providing little new information. If your hypotheses are being only somewhat validated, you'll have to decide whether to keep iterating on hypotheses before moving on to the next step, or to proceed while continuing primary market research in parallel to develop better hypotheses.

As you go through the steps, you will be continually refining your hypotheses for greater specificity, and you will keep learning about the target customer, so do not think you must have the "perfect" answer before moving on. There are no perfect answers, and forward progress through the 24 Steps is the only way you will be able to rigorously test your assumptions. Sometimes you reach a limit on primary market research where you have to take more concrete steps like a prototype or even a Minimum Viable Business Product (MVBP).

As I mentioned before, people can say one thing—and really mean it—but then do something completely different, so do not expect that your interviews will accurately reflect the person's willingness to become a paying customer. Trust but verify the results. When money changes hands, the credibility of your results increase dramatically.

Toward the end, Step 23, you will be setting up a unified full systems test for the MVBP, which will be the ultimate test for your product. It is likely you will find many surprises—or as I call them, learning opportunities!—when you build the MVBP. But your goal is to find as many of these surprises earlier, especially ones that can be fatal if caught too late in the process. That is why throughout the 24 Steps, you formulate and test hypotheses at almost every step. Good primary market research is essential to validating or invalidating hypotheses quickly so you spend more time building products that customers want.

Tools of Primary Market Research

The tools of primary market research may seem like a longer list than it actually is. At the end of the day, an entrepreneur has limited time and resources. No one is as invested in a product's design and success as the core team is, so at the start, virtually all of the primary market research has to be done by the founding team. It is very difficult and dangerous to outsource primary market research. You would never outsource your eyes, ears, and brain to someone else, and certainly not in an innovation-driven startup like you envision creating.

The real gold in many cases is not your product, but rather the knowledge you have gained working with the new customers in this emerging market opportunity, since you will know their needs, wants, and context better than anyone else. This is why it is so crucial, when starting your company, that you deal directly with your customers. See firsthand how they like, use, dislike, and misuse your product.

I will talk more about this in Step 18, Map the Sales Process to Acquire a Customer, but I learned a very important lesson from IBM when I got trained there at the start of my career. They said, "Whoever owns the customer owns everything." That is especially sage advice for a new product in an emerging market.

Here are several methods that entrepreneurs have used for primary market research:

1. **Customer interviews:** As noted above, this is the most common. Essential for qualitative and also good for quantitative.

2. **Observational research:** Watch customers do their work. Potentially, you would videorecord them or record their mouse and keyboard activity. You would ride with them in the passenger seat (real or metaphorically) as they do their job, carefully observing and asking questions at the right time while making sure not to change their behavior through your actions or questions.

3. **Immersion:** Do the customer's work and fully experience all the dimensions of the job in a way that will give you an understanding that may not come from observation.

4. **User tests:** Landing pages and the like don't just draw in candidates but also give important insights into their behavior and preferences. A/B testing is another form of this and can be very effective, especially if it can be done digitally.

5. **Focus groups:** This is another traditional tool that people refer to but has become less and less enthusiastically embraced by entrepreneurs. It can be useful, especially if done very carefully, but it can also have lots of biases and is expensive.

6. **User-driven innovation:** This is a technique described and validated through research by MIT Sloan Entrepreneurship Professor Eric von Hippel. It encourages you to look for the end user with the most acute pain from the problem and see how they are finding or developing a workaround solution.

7. **Outcome-driven innovation:** This framework is also known as "Jobs to Be Done," created by Anthony Ulwick and popularized by Harvard Business School Professor Clayton Christensen. Outcome-driven innovation is based on the concept that customers have measurable outcomes they are trying to achieve in their day-to-day (aka when they are doing a job), and a company should link its innovation to those customer outcomes because customers buy products to get jobs done.

In the end, because entrepreneurs don't have much time or money, they focus on 1–4. They might do some other creative things, like a mystery shop of the closest product (I want to encourage this and other creative ideas). For sure, focus groups are falling out of favor with entrepreneurs, with reason. The methodology of 6 and 7 offer interesting alternatives to creative entrepreneurs, and understanding them to make tools 1–4 better designed and more effective is time well spent.

Primary market research is an imperfect process and can be messy, but it is critically important.

References and Resources

- *Talking to Humans* by Giff Constable: If you read one book on this topic, it should be this one. Very easy read and yet packed with practical knowledge about how to do interviews.

- User Innovation edX course with Professor Eric von Hippel: Excellent, easy way to get knowledge from the originator of the concept. Great content and examples that make the fundamental concept easy to understand and apply. The online class is available at https://www.edx.org/course/user-innovation-path-entrepreneurship-mitx-uinov8x-0; he also has a website with extensive free downloadable information at https://evhippel.mit.edu/books/.

- Elaine Chen's portfolio of primary market research materials: Elaine is on the MIT faculty and our go-to practitioner for doing primary market research. She has a long history of doing ethnographic research and using it to build products, both working at startups and as a consultant to other startups. Here is a list of her easy-to-read yet very practical materials:

  - "3 Go-to Techniques for Primary Market Research," *Huffington Post*, http://www.huffingtonpost.com/entry/three-go-to-techniques-for-primary-market-research_us_577d4001e4b0746f5648b963

  - "How Startups Can Run Better Landing Page Tests," *Xconomy*, http://www.xconomy.com/boston/2016/04/07/how-startups-can-run-better-landing-page-tests/

  - "A Primer on Primary Market Research," http://www.slideshare.net/chenelaine/primary-market-research-an-overview-on-qualitative-and-quantitative-research-techniques

  - Templates and samples:
    - Research protocol template: http://www.slideshare.net/secret/epzen6sYi1gWGr
    - Sample discussion guide: http://www.slideshare.net/secret/d4a2d3FzWdDnNU
    - Sample recruitment questionnaire: http://www.slideshare.net/secret/iIMMrhNvWJhv1h
    - Sample recruitment form for internal use: http://www.slideshare.net/secret/JzXpLWZmlLoAGq

- Jobs-To-Be-Done: See http://strategyn.com/customer-centered-innovation-map/ as a starting point.

WORSHEETS

The Primary Market Research Pledge

I have all of my students sign this pledge at the beginning of the semester before they start to work on their projects. You should also fully commit yourself to proper primary market research by having each member of your team sign this pledge.

PLEDGE TO SERVE THE INTERESTS OF THE CUSTOMER

I do hereby solemnly swear to follow the lead of potential customers in the pursuit of a product and/or service while starting and building my start-up.

I recognize that I am subject to confirmation bias, and as such will approach primary market research as an opportunity to question assumptions and to search for different alternatives.

I understand that it is not a sign of weakness, lack of intellect, or other shortcoming to modify or completely change the idea with which I started. In fact, I acknowledge that failing to make adjustments is a likely sign of confirmation bias. When we discover new information, we must be willing to change.

This does not mean it is the customer's job to design the product, because that job is mine. But I will seek to honestly understand the customers' needs, wants, pain points, pressures, opportunities, and much more to design a solution that will create great value for them and minimize any friction it takes for them to adopt it.

Print name: _____

Signature: _____

Date: _____

Primary Market Research Worksheet I: Preparation
Make a new copy of this worksheet for each market segment you analyze.

1. **Secondary market research sources and key lessons learned:**

   a _____

   _____

   _____

   b. _____

   _____

   _____

   c. _____

   _____

   _____

2. **Profile(s) of the people you want to engage with** (e.g., description of end user, economic buyer, champion, industry analysts, influencers; description should be enough to help you identify, find, and deselect potential candidates. Can include demographics and psychographics—see Step 3 for more info):

   1st Targeted Profile Name: _____

   Description: _____

   _____

   2nd Targeted Profile Name: _____

   Description: _____

   _____

   3rd Targeted Profile Name: _____

   Description: _____

   _____

   4th Targeted Profile Name: _____

   Description: _____

   _____

   5th Targeted Profile Name: _____

   Description: _____

   _____

3. **Your general recruitment script (be clear on who you are, why you want to engage, what you are asking for):**

   _____

   _____

   _____

   _____

4.   **Initial candidate list to contact**

Name & contact info	Profile type	Source	Why you want to engage with this person plus any other info to build rapport

Primary Market Research Worksheet II: Execution

Make a new copy of this worksheet for each market segment you analyze.

1. **Which profile are you engaging with:** _____

   How well does this person fit the profile: _____

   Type of engagement (e.g., interview, observation, test, immersion, other): _____

2. **Your general script/framework for engagement (Guidance: open-ended → qualitative insights/hypotheses → [if appropriate] quantitative insights/hypotheses and data) (approximately 5 key items):**

   a. _____

   b. _____

   c. _____

   d _____

   e. _____

3. **What did you learn?**

4. **What surprised you?**

5. **Which hypotheses did you seem to confirm? How and why?**

6. **Which hypotheses did you seem to invalidate? How and why?**

_____
_____
_____
_____

7. **Which hypotheses were you unable to reach conclusions on? Why?**

_____
_____
_____
_____

8. **What new questions were raised in this engagement?**

_____
_____
_____
_____

9. **List of additional future candidates obtained from current candidate**

Name & contact info	Profile type	Why does the current candidate think we should engage with this person, plus any other info to build rapport

10. **What changes should I make for the next primary market research engagement?**

    Profile changes: _____

    _____

    Qualitative insights/hypotheses updated (could be more or less than 3):

    a. _____

    _____

    b. _____

    _____

    c. _____

    _____

Quantitative insights/hypotheses updated (optional—only if appropriate and you are far enough along) (could be more or less than 3):

a. _____

_____

b. _____

_____

c. _____

_____

Script update:

a. _____

_____

_____

b. _____

_____

_____

c. _____

_____

_____

d. _____

_____

_____

11. **Headline for this engagement:**

_____

_____

_____

_____

STEP 2

Select a Beachhead Market

WHAT IS STEP 2, SELECT A BEACHHEAD MARKET?

Select one market segment from the Market Segmentation analysis, Step 1, to be the first market your business will focus on to achieve initial business success.

WHY DO WE DO THIS STEP, AND WHY DO WE DO IT NOW?

As a new entity, you have limited resources, so focusing those resources is essential. You do this step now because, now that you have completed at least a first pass Market Segmentation, you can start to intelligently concentrate your efforts on a single market segment to make better and faster progress.

By the Book: See pages 41–45 of *Disciplined Entrepreneurship* for basic knowledge on this step.
See pages 45–47 of *Disciplined Entrepreneurship* for examples of how different companies and teams have addressed this step.

"PERSON WHO CHASES TWO RABBITS CATCHES NEITHER"

— ROMANIAN PROVERB

PROCESS GUIDE

The *Merriam-Webster Dictionary* defines beachhead as "a beach on an enemy's shore that an invading army takes and controls in order to prepare for the arrival of more soldiers and supplies." The analogy for entrepreneurs is that to optimize your chances of success in a timely manner, you will employ the same game plan, choosing a small market segment you can control until your company has sufficient resources to enter other markets.

First, ask yourself: Are the markets from your Market Segmentation in Step 1 well-defined enough and small enough to attack successfully and not only conquer, but dominate? You will compare each market against the three conditions that define a market, which I have refined from *Disciplined Entrepreneurship* and focused on the end user:

1. **Same product:** The end users will all use the same product. If you have to make slightly different products to appeal to the different end users in your market, it's too broad of a market.

2. **Same sales process:** The sales process to the end users will be the same, meaning interchangeable language, value proposition, sales channels, etc. If your salespeople have to change tactics from one end user to the next, your market's not targeted enough!

3. **Word of mouth:** There is strong word of mouth between end users in this community. If your end users don't talk to each other—if they are separated by large distances, for example—you're going to have a hard time building up sales across the full group of end users. Refine it!

Use the Market Segmentation Certification worksheet at the end of this chapter to analyze the markets from your Market Segmentation, then go back and refine your markets if necessary—it's almost always a requirement to further segment your markets.

Once your Market Segmentation is sufficiently refined, it's time to choose your Beachhead Market. A few tips:

- Involve the whole founding team. Presumably you've already refined the composition of your team somewhat in Step 1; continue to do so here. You want to finish this step with increased cohesion on your team. You also want to identify and address any team dynamics issues. You haven't worked together much, so you'll likely have some issues. Be honest about them, and recognize and address them professionally. If you don't do it now, you'll pay a steeper and steeper price as time goes on—in my experience, failure to address team issues up front is the number one reason companies fail. The hardest part of a startup is not technology or strategy, it's people.

- Avoid "analysis paralysis." There is almost always more than one path to success. Your goal is to eliminate the paths with the lowest odds of success, and choose one path with relatively good odds. Then, take your chosen path and pursue it without thinking about "what could've been"— burn the boats! Pursue it until it proves not to work or is much less attractive than originally anticipated.

- Keep doing primary market research! Part of why you narrow your selections is because primary market research is time consuming and expensive in terms of opportunity costs, so you want to focus your research on compelling candidates for Beachhead Market. But don't stop doing primary market research just because your Market Segmentation is done. In fact, you have only just begun!

You'll consider the same seven key criteria that you used during the Step 1 Market Segmentation:

1. Is the target customer well-funded?
2. Is the target customer readily accessible to your sales force?
3. Does the target customer have a compelling reason to buy?
4. Can you deliver a whole product?
5. Is there entrenched competition?
6. Can you leverage this market segment to enter others?
7. Is the market consistent with the values, passions, and goals of the team?

Use the Beachhead Market Selection worksheet to compile your notes on your potential Beachhead Markets and to rank and make a decision about which will be your beachhead. It may take a number of iterations, and you might not end up being right with your ultimate selection. But if you later determine your selection will not work, you can always come back (much more easily than if an army chooses the wrong beachhead!) and restart at this point with more confidence and skill in executing the process. For now, you want a good amount of confidence that your structured analysis and plentiful primary market research have brought you to this reasonable decision.

Finally, before you move on to the next step, all of your team members must sign the Agreement on the Beachhead Market Selection. It is important that everyone is on the same page (literally!) and that they are enthusiastically behind the direction your company will be going in. Companies that thrive in their Beachhead Markets are companies with strong cohesion and unity.

———

GENERAL EXERCISES TO UNDERSTAND CONCEPT

See the back of the book for answers to these questions.

1. In World War II, what was the beachhead for the Allies as they invaded Nazi-controlled Western Europe? Why was this a good beachhead? Where did the Allied forces go from there (i.e., what were their "follow-on markets"?)

   _____

   _____

   _____

2. What was the Beachhead Market for Facebook?

   _____

   _____

   _____

3. For Pinterest?

   _____

   _____

   _____

4. For desktop computers in businesses?

   _____

   _____

   _____

5. For Apple?

   _____

   _____

   _____

6. For the first cell phones?

   _____

   _____

   _____

WORKSHEETS

Market Segmentation Certification Worksheet

a. Are all market segments actually market segments in that they meet all of the three criteria for a market (similar product, similar sales process, word of mouth)?

___ Yes   ___ No

b. Do your market segments identify actual human end users and not just general companies or department in companies?

___ Yes   ___ No

c. Are the market segments segmented down into reasonable sizes for your start-up to address (i.e., less than a billion and more than a few hundred thousand)? (More on this later in Step 4.)

___ Yes   ___ No

d. Are these criteria met? If these criteria are not met, then continue to iterate on the market segmentation matrix until they are.

___ Yes, then done   ___ No, then iterate (return)

e. Understand that your first Market Segmentation Analysis does not have to be correct; it will certainly have lots of holes in it, but make an intellectually honest attempt (i.e., without biases as much as possible) to answer the fundamental questions in the matrix as best you can. Only then can you make an educated guess on what the top Beachhead Markets are to analyze further.

___ I understand, and now I can proceed.

Beachhead Market Selection Worksheet

Criteria	Market Segment = _____	Market Segment = _____	Market Segment = _____	Market Segment = _____
	Rating is Very High (best), High, Medium, Low, Show Stopper (worst)			
1. Economically attractive				
2. Accessible to your sales force				
3. Strong value proposition				
4. Complete product				
5. Competition				
6. Strategic value				
7. Personal alignment				
Overall rating				
	Rating for ranking is 1 (most attractive) to 4 (least attractive) – key factors is most important contributor to the ranking			
Ranking				
Key deciding factors				

DECISION FOR TEAM TO SIGN OFF ON THE BEACHHEAD MARKET

AGREEMENT ON THE BEACHHEAD MARKET SELECTION

We have systematically analyzed the various potential market segments and arrived at a decision for one beachhead market (not more than one). We each understand that in real life, there is always more than one path to success. The key is to choose one that will work and avoid those that will not work—but choose one and get going on it! As such, we each understand that we are not going to be locked into a state of analysis paralysis whereby we are going to try to take out all the risk in this decision because that is not possible. We will also not spend unnecessary time trying to determine which of the successful paths is slightly better than the others because there are so many unknowns.

But what is possible is to focus on one and only one market, and that is what we are going to do. We have deselected all the other market segments and will not be distracted by them. I will personally do this, and I will also hold my teammates accountable and point out when the team starts to get distracted. If a teammate points this out to me, then I will listen carefully and refocus if I am the cause of the distraction.

As such, each of us does by solemnly swear that we will focus on the _____ market segment and pursue it until we fully achieve our objectives (e.g., market leader, cash flow positive in this market segment, etc.) or until it has been further segmented or until we have proven that it is not viable. If we do switch, we will do it as a team and then give the new market our focus, but until such time, we will be completely committed to one and only one market segment, the one noted above.

Team Member #1: Signature _____ Name _____ Date _____

Team Member #2: Signature _____ Name _____ Date _____

Team Member #3: Signature _____ Name _____ Date _____

Team Member #4: Signature _____ Name _____ Date _____

Team Member #5: Signature _____ Name _____ Date _____

STEP 3

Build an End User Profile for the Beachhead Market

WHAT IS STEP 3, BUILD AN END USER PROFILE FOR THE BEACHHEAD MARKET?

Using primary market research techniques, build out a description, including demographic and psychographic information, with specific facts about the end users of your product. You will include their needs and wants as well as invaluable information about their behavior.

WHY DO WE DO THIS STEP, AND WHY DO WE DO IT NOW?

There are three reasons you do this step:

1. To keep the focus on the customer
2. To validate your selection of Beachhead Market by deepening your understanding of the end user
3. To provide the necessary information to estimate the Total Addressable Market (TAM) in the next step

---

By the Book: See pages 49–53 of *Disciplined Entrepreneurship* for basic knowledge on this step. See pages 53–56 of *Disciplined Entrepreneurship* for examples of how different companies and teams have addressed this step.

I can generally see them and describe them to you, but they are not in completely clear focus yet.

Building the End User Profile brings the focus to the actual person who uses your product, so that real value is created by your product.

PROCESS GUIDE

Once you have identified your Beachhead Market, you need to dive in and do a detailed analysis of the market to see if it is in fact viable, see if you have scoped it out and defined it properly, and start to develop a game plan to effectively "attack" this market.

As I describe more fully in *Disciplined Entrepreneurship*, the customer is not a monolithic being, but consists of a number of people playing different roles, particularly when selling to a business. Even if a person both uses the product ("end user") and makes the decision to purchase the product ("primary economic buyer"), there may be a range of other individuals involved in the decision, and you'll fully explore that in Step 12, Determine the Customer's Decision-Making Unit.

You will start analyzing the customer for this market by developing the End User Profile. Why start with the end user and not the person who will pay? Because if the end user does not use your product, the customer realizes no value in buying your product and nobody will pay you for it. If by chance someone does pay you once, they won't buy again. In either case, you will not have an economically sustainable business.

This workbook focuses on one-sided markets, where only one kind of end user is required for the product to work, so that you have a good grounding in the fundamental principles of building an End User Profile. Multisided markets, such as marketplace platforms like eBay that attract both buyers and sellers, use the same techniques described herein, but they require developing an End User Profile for each side of the market.

The fundamental concept of the End User Profile is that it must be a person and not an organization or department. In the end, it is a human being, or set of human beings, who will use your product or oversee the use of your product, so you need to deeply understand this person, or as I say in class, you must "walk a few miles in their shoes."

There are six items that are the most common when building a useful End User Profile. You may want to expand or contract this list depending on the complexity and economics of your situation.

1. **Demographics:** Demographics are quantifiable data that can be used to identify your target end user and also filter out those who are not your end user. These are things like gender, age, income, geographic location, level of education, school attended, and other relatively easily measurable factors. The good news is that these are pretty easy to figure out, but the bad news is that they might not always be useful in understanding your end user. Knowing your end users are women in their 20s, even if you narrow the group down to a certain income group and geographic location, does not gain you much information if there exist wildly divergent attitudes, values, or fears in that group. As a result, the demographics are becoming less important than the psychographics. Definitely analyze the demographics, but then decide how much emphasis to put on them as you move forward. Use the worksheet below and sources online to customize which demographics you collect for your situation.

2. **Psychographics:** *Merriam-Webster Dictionary* defines psychographics as "market research or statistics classifying population groups according to psychological variables (as attitudes, values, or fears)." The simple working definition I give in class is that psychographics refers to the qualitative description of your target end users. What are their aspirations? Who are their heroes? Understand how they behave based on what they believe, rather than the general identifiable characteristics that demographics give you. Psychographics are immensely valuable but are much harder to get or analyze. Lots of government or industry database services, or even Facebook, can break down information by age, geography, industry or job classification, or income, but far fewer can be searched by "number one fear."

3. **Proxy Product:** What products do these end users also buy today? This information is valuable because it shows how the end users already behave, instead of how they might theoretically behave if your product were to exist. Sometimes, proxy products are complementary products. If someone owns a Lexus automobile (a high-end and expensive but high-quality car), they would likely buy an expensive but high-quality brand of tires like Michelin. Other times, proxy products demonstrate similar demographic and psychographic characteristics. If someone buys a Toyota Prius, a hybrid gas-electric car that is more expensive than Toyota's Camry sedan, they are indicating that they are likely interested in mitigating their environmental impact and that they have enough money to act on that passion. They are likely good candidates to also own, or at least be very interested in, solar panels.

4. **Watering Holes:** Watering holes are the places where your end users congregate and exchange information. They are reliable places for information about your product to be spread by "word of mouth," which is far more effective than advertising. They also provide some corroboration for your demographic and psychographic information because you can infer things about people by the company they keep. The forms that watering holes take can be very diverse in nature as they can be industry conferences, Saturday morning soccer fields, bars (literal watering holes), online platforms, and many others.

5. **Day in the Life:** Literally tell the story of what it is like to walk in your end user's shoes for a typical day. In this step, since you have not yet focused on one end user you will call the Persona, the "day in the life" will be a composite—but make it a composite of multiple end users

whom you have actually spent a day observing and talking with. The resulting story sets aside abstract studies and statistics and brings it all home to your team by helping them understand what happens in real life. It also reinforces and helps you refine the rest of your End User Profile.

6. **Biggest Fears and Motivators:** What keeps your end users awake at night more than anything else? What are your customers' top priorities—their fears and motivators? I don't mean with relation to the product you're hoping they will buy; I mean in general. When you do your primary market research, sit with end users and make a comprehensive list of all their concerns. Then, ask them to weight their priorities by giving more points to higher priorities, with a total of 100 points across all the priorities. This exercise forces prioritization. As part of the End User Profile, you'll want a weighted list of your end user's top five or so priorities. Confirm this list with the end users you talk to as much as possible. This list will be extremely useful going forward.

Your primary market research from previous steps may be useful here, but you will likely need to do additional primary market research to complete your End User Profile. Don't guess or make stereotypical judgments about what your End User Profile "should" look like in an attempt to save time. In the end, you want information about real people, because it's real people who will use your product, not fictional characters in a marketing document.

GENERAL EXERCISES TO UNDERSTAND CONCEPT

1. Pick a successful product that you know well. Who do you think the target end user is for that product? Write down the demographics and psychographics, and be as specific as you can.

   Demographics (your guess): _____

   Psychographics (your guess): _____

   Now go to the product's website, look up advertisements for the product in the media, and see if the message there is consistent with your profile. Do the end users depicted look like what you expect them to? Is the product appealing to the priorities of your profile?

   Demographics (per website/ads): _____

   Psychographics (per website/ads): _____

   What messages, images, proxy products, and other factors give you hints as to the product's End User Profile?

   _____

   _____

2. Politicians and their teams are extremely aware of "end voter" profiles. Pick two candidates who are competing directly against each other in a current or recent election, and try to define each candidate's "base," their core group of voters, which is analogous to a Beachhead Market. In doing so, look at the candidates' contrasting messages and images and notice how they reassure and attract these people to the candidate.

	Candidate 1:	Candidate 2:
Demographics of base:		
Psychographics of base:		
"Proxy products"—what things do members of the base actually do in their lives that demonstrate they might be inclined to support the candidate?		
What watering holes do members of the base frequent?		
What is the biggest fear or motivator of their base?		

——————

WORKSHEET

End User Profile for Beachhead Market

Demographics (be sure to determine which are relevant for your situation, but some general categories are gender, age, income, geography, job title, education, ethnicity, marital status, political affiliations, etc.)	
Psychographics (as above, this needs to be customized for your situation, but examples are aspirations, fears, motivators, hobbies, opinions, values, life priorities, personality traits, habits, etc.)	
Proxy Products (what other products do these end users own and which do they value the most? Which products have the highest correlation with your target end users?)	
Watering Holes (e.g., locations, associations, online platforms—and sequence them in priority and indicate intensity of each)	
Day in the Life (describe a day in the life of the end user and what is going on in his or her head)	
Priorities (what are your end user's priorities, and assign a weighting to each so that it adds up to 100)	_____ Weighting: _____ _____ Weighting: _____ _____ Weighting: _____ _____ Weighting: _____ _____ Weighting: _____

Now that you know the profile of the end user, you can assess future interactions you have with potential customers to determine whether they are actually in your End User Profile and are worth your time. If they do not fit the profile, engaging with their needs will distract you from building a great product to meet a specific customer pain. And you can now estimate how many end users exist in your market, which leads you directly to Step 4, Estimate the Total Addressable Market (TAM) for the Beachhead Market.

STEP 4

Estimate the Total Addressable Market (TAM) for the Beachhead Market

WHAT IS STEP 4, ESTIMATE THE TOTAL ADDRESSABLE MARKET (TAM) FOR THE BEACHHEAD MARKET?

Estimating the TAM is a process to estimate the total revenue you could achieve (in units of dollars per year) in your Beachhead Market if you achieved 100 percent market share.

WHY DO WE DO THIS STEP, AND WHY DO WE DO IT NOW?

The TAM needs to be an appropriate size for your new venture. Too big and you won't be able to mobilize enough resources to compete; too small and your company won't have enough revenue to sustain itself. The exercise of calculating the TAM also increases your team's knowledge of the market. Beyond just a simple number, your team will exit this step understanding what makes the selected Beachhead Market attractive. This understanding may be more important than your TAM size and a simple "go/no go" decision.

> **By the Book:** See pages 57–61 of *Disciplined Entrepreneurship* for basic knowledge on this step. See pages 61–67 of *Disciplined Entrepreneurship* for examples of how different companies and teams have addressed this step.

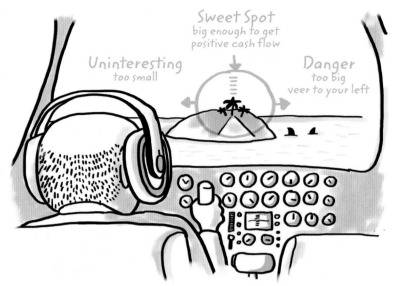

Beachhead TAM calculation
is your sanity check
that you are headed
in the right direction

PROCESS GUIDE

To calculate the TAM, you will do the following:

- Estimate the number of end users in the Beachhead Market, using a combination of top-down and bottom-up analysis.
- Estimate the annual revenue that each end user is worth to your company.

The TAM will be helpful in determining whether your Beachhead Market is too big or too small[1], but remember that it is a general estimate. You should not present it as a precise number. It is extremely important to always show your assumptions so that others can understand your logic.

The TAM is also a good way for your team to understand the broader context of the Beachhead Market. The previous and subsequent steps are all about narrowing your focus, so this step allows you to take in the larger picture of what you are looking to achieve.

---

[1] In *Disciplined Entrepreneurship* on page 60, I state that if "your TAM is less than $5 million per year it is possible that your new venture has not identified a big enough Beachhead Market." I would like to emphasize and clarify that the lower end number was a very general guideline and was in the context of the United States. You should feel free to entertain smaller markets, but think carefully if you are being ambitious enough in the long term. Many have rightfully justified smaller markets, especially outside the United States.

Start by estimating the number of end users in the Beachhead Market. You will use a combination of top-down analysis (based on secondary market research) and bottom-up analysis sometimes called "counting noses"—counting the number of end users one by one). Since bottom-up analysis is more difficult, I have reserved that process guide for the "Advanced" section at the end of this chapter.

In a top-down analysis, you will use the criteria from your end user profile from Step 3 to locate secondary research that helps you demonstrate how many end users exist. In particular, the criteria from the demographics, proxy products, and watering holes categories are the easiest to use for this analysis.

You are unlikely to find one secondary source that matches all your criteria. Therefore, select a few key criteria (try to simplify to four or fewer) that help you narrow down the information the secondary sources give you. For instance, how many schoolteachers own two houses? You may need to pull the number of multiple-house owners, and the number of schoolteachers, and figure out an intelligent way to combine the numbers based on other estimates. Refer to the OnDemandKorea example in *Disciplined Entrepreneurship* (pages 64–76) if you are unsure of where to start.

Fill out the Top-Down Estimate worksheet with your criteria and number of end users, along with an explanation of the assumptions you are making.

Next, determine how much revenue each end user is worth to you each year. This part's tougher. Remember you're not determining the price of your product (that starts in Step 16); you're making a first pass estimate on the customer's willingness and ability to pay for a solution. Don't indicate precision that you clearly do not have, but instead focus on getting an order of magnitude.

Here are three good ways to start an estimate on the annualized revenue per end user:

1. **What the customer currently spends.** The customer is likely spending money already to try to solve the customer pain, or spends money on a product that causes the customer pain and your product would replace. You'll want to know:

   - How much does each product cost?

   - How many of each product does the customer buy for the end user?

   - What is the average lifetime of the product before it's replaced?

      The annualized revenue is the total cost per end user of the product(s) the customer buys for the end user, divided by the lifetime. For instance, if each customer buys one automobile at $15,000 that lasts for five years, the annualized revenue is $15,000 / 5 = $3,000.

2. **The customer's available budget.** Think about the following:

   - When you look at the market today, how much is being spent overall to solve the problem that you are looking to solve for a typical user?

   - How much money does the customer have (household income, business revenue, etc.)?

   - What fraction of that amount could you see being allocated to solve this problem?

3. **Comparables.** Comparables are similar products or data points in different markets that you can use to bolster your TAM analysis. There will be no exact comparable, as you are doing something new, but often you can find companies that provide data points that are close enough to what you intend to do that they are very valuable. For instance, if you are creating a product whose revenue is supported by advertising, what are current advertising rates for similar demographics to your end user? Comparables require some creative thinking, but they can be extremely valuable to sanity-check your other TAM estimates.

After you have come up with these various data points, triangulate against them and make a judgment call as to what you think is the appropriate range at this point. Remember, you will not get this precisely right, so the key is to spend enough time to make an informed guess at this point without investing a tremendous amount of time and effort (it is important to keep moving) and then revisit it later.

Other Important Considerations for TAM

The single number of the TAM is a simplification to give you a quick sense of the magnitude of your Beachhead Market. Before you draw a final conclusion from this number, there are some other important factors you should consider:

- **Profitability**: How profitable is the revenue? Is it software where the profitability is essentially over 99 percent? This will make your TAM size more attractive. Or is it a commodity like energy where your profitability on the revenue could be 10 percent or even less? That makes the number much less attractive. In most businesses, your goal in the Beachhead Market is to get to positive cash flow if possible prior to expanding to adjacent markets.

- **Time to Conquer Market**: How long will it take to succeed or fail in this market? Is it a mobile app that will likely succeed or not in six months? That is good. Or rather, is it more like a medical device or new drug where it will take years to learn your fate? That is a negative consideration.

- **Compound Annual Growth Rate (CAGR) of Overall Revenue**: Is this a market that is just starting up and has great growth potential? That would be a positive factor. Or is it a mature market where users have set habits and the total market size is in decline? That would be a negative factor.

- **Anticipated Market Share**: Is this a winner-take-all market driven by networking effects? That could be a positive factor if you have a strong competitive position. Or is it a market that will have many players and no player will get more than a small fraction of the market? That would be a negative factor.

There are other considerations as well (such as how much investment will be required, what is the strength of the current entrenched "competitor"—a lot of that would have also come up in the Beachhead Market selection process in Step 2), but this is sufficient to have a good dialogue with your team. While the TAM size and the other considerations are important in determining whether a Beachhead Market is well-defined enough to proceed or not, do not forget the seven factors in Step 2 that led you to choose the initial market segment you did. The size of the market is just one dimension to evaluate when determining how confident you are in your selection of Beachhead Market. You are balancing the TAM size with the odds of success and the strategic value of the market (i.e., how well this market will strengthen your Core and how well it positions you for follow-on markets).

___

GENERAL EXERCISES TO UNDERSTAND CONCEPT

1. What do you think the TAM is for toothbrushes in the United States? What assumptions did you make in calculating it?

_____

_____

_____

_____

2. Now what would you estimate as the TAM in the United States for high-quality electric toothbrushes that cost $150? What assumptions did you make in calculating it?

_____

_____

_____

_____

3. What are the biggest unknowns in your assumptions that you would need to research further?

_____

_____

_____

_____

WORKSHEETS

Top-Down Estimate of Number of End Users in Beachhead Market

Number of people in your largest demographic or psychographic characteristic = _____

Based on End User Profile characteristic: _____
Assumption(s): _____
_____
Source(s): _____
_____

1st segmentation based on end user profile = _____

Based on End User Profile characteristic: _____
% of previous segment: _____ %
Assumption(s) for calculation: _____
Source(s): _____
_____

2nd segmentation based on end user profile = _____

Based on End User Profile characteristic: _____
% of previous segment: _____ %
Assumption(s) for calculation: _____
Source(s): _____
_____

3rd segmentation based on end user profile = _____

Based on End User Profile characteristic: _____
% of previous segment: _____ %
Assumption(s) for calculation: _____
Source(s): _____
_____

End users in beachhead market = _____

Based on End User Profile characteristic: _____
% of previous segment: _____ %
Assumption(s) for calculation: _____
Source(s): _____
_____

I.	One Time Charge Data Point	
Ia	Estimation of price per unit	
Ib	Number of units needed per end user	
Ic	Average life of product in years	
Id	Annualized revenue (Ia*Ib)/Id (Data Point I)	
2.	Budget Available Data Points	
2a	Current spending per end user (Data Point 2)	
2b	Total budget for the end user	
2c	What percentage of budget could go to this solution reasonably?	
2d	Annualize revenue (2b*2c) (Data Point 3)	
3.	Comparables	
3a	Who are the comparables for your business?	
3b	What are the comparable products?	
3c	What is the comparable converted to similar annualized revenue (Data Point 4 plus however many more you deem relevant)?	
4.	Interpreting the Results	
4a	Consensus on estimate of annualized revenue per end user, based on the four Data Points above (a range is fine)	
	How did you end up at this number/range?	

The final items beyond Beachhead Market TAM are the other dimensions that are important to provide more meaning to the overall number. A $10 million Beachhead Market TAM that has 99 percent profitability where you can win 100 percent market share in less than a year, which also happens to be growing at 30 percent a year, is totally different than a $10 million Beachhead Market TAM with 10 percent profitability where you will only get 10 percent market share after three years of effort and the market is shrinking each year.

This information should be collected and then added in to fill out the Top-Down TAM Analysis Summary below to give a robust sense of the economic attractiveness of market characteristics of the Beachhead Market.

Top-Down TAM Analysis Summary

1	Total # of end users in the broad market segment		Source/ based on:	
2	Total # of end users in the targeted subsegment of your Beachhead Market		Source/ based on:	
3	Annual monetizable revenue per end user		Source/ based on:	
4	Estimate of top-down TAM (line 2 times line 3)			
5	Estimate of range of profitability for your product		Source/ based on:	
6	Estimated Compound Annual Growth Rate (CAGR)		Source/ based on:	
7	Estimated time to achieve 20 percent market share		Source/ based on:	
8	Anticipated market share achieved if you are reasonably successful		Source/ based on:	
	What are the three top assumptions that could affect the attractiveness of the Beachhead Market for your product (besides the product itself)?	1. _____ _____ 2. _____ _____ 3. _____		

Based on this summary analysis, use the checklist below to assess whether your Beachhead Market is a good size:

Checklist after TAM Analysis of Beachhead Market

		Yes	No
1	Is the market big enough to be interesting?		
2	Is it reasonable in size for us to achieve meaningful word of mouth, meaning it is not too big?		
3	Is it possible to get to positive cash flow in this market in a reasonable period of time (typically three years, but it might be shorter or longer depending on the industry)? Note: This question takes into consideration the extra four factors described above.		
4	Do we still feel good about this Beachhead Market as our initial market?		

If the answer to any of these is no, consider carefully before you move forward. Many of the high-profile entrepreneurs who have access to significant investment capital, or have a very strong personal balance sheet themselves, can ignore #3, but I would advise you not to ignore this question otherwise. It might be the second most important question for your survival. The most important question is the last one, because if you don't feel good about this market, you need to figure out why.

ADVANCED TOPICS: BOTTOM-UP TAM ANALYSIS

As mentioned, a bottom-up analysis is extremely powerful and gives you invaluable insights that are not generally possible through secondary research. Bottom-up analysis is also very time consuming and difficult to get information for. If you are unsure about your market or your commitment to this idea, skip this part and come back later when you are more confident about your Beachhead Market and have a deeper understanding of the market. Most plans rely on top-down analysis, and while I think it's insufficient, it is the reality that bottom-up analysis is much, much harder to do.

The below worksheet uses a concept called "end user density" that allows you to complete a bottom-up analysis without the need to identify every single end user in a market, since that process can be prohibitively expensive in terms of time consumed.

To calculate end user density, you'll first need some way to divide up the market into countable units. For instance, in the SensAble example in *Disciplined Entrepreneurship*, we sold to companies that employed industrial designers, and they defined their countable entity as overall number of employees. Their resulting "designer density" for their market was expressed as the number of designers per thousand employees.

For a consumer product, your countable unit could be population, a specific socioeconomic segment of the population, the number of people who own another product, and so on. For businesses it may be number of employees, revenue, products released each year, number of customers that company has, and the like. These units depend on your situation. Clever choice of countable unit for density will give credibility to your TAM estimate, so spend some time to optimize your choice on this unit, understanding it is still an estimate.

Once you have defined your countable unit, go to three instances of this unit and "count noses," determining exactly how many end users are within that countable unit. Also determine how many people overall are in that countable unit.

Then, for each instance, determine what the annualized revenue per end user is, based on the unique circumstances of each instance. Do not guess; ask the people from this instance of the countable unit!

Bottom-Up TAM Analysis Worksheet

What countable unit are you using for end user density? _____

What are three instances (i.e., real, verifiable examples) of this countable unit you will be using to "count noses"?

1. _____
2. _____
3. _____

	Instance 1= _____	Instance 2= _____	Instance 3= _____
Who did you speak to in order to gather this info?			
# of end users			
# of people in the countable unit			
Density ratio (# end users / # people in countable unit)			
How representative of the whole market do you believe this instance is?			
In this instance, what is your estimate of the annualized revenue per end user?			

Based on the above table, what is the reasonable estimate of the end user density? _____

What is the reasonable estimate of the annualized revenue per end user? _____

Based on the end user density, what is the reasonable estimate for the number of end users in the market? _____

What is the reasonable estimate for the TAM (# end users multiplied by annualized revenue per end user)? _____

Four additional factors to consider:		
Estimate of range of profitability for your product:	Based on:	Confidence Level:
Estimated compound annual growth rate (CAGR):	Based on:	Confidence Level:
Estimated time to achieve 20 percent market share:	Based on:	Confidence Level:
Anticipated market share achieved if you are reasonably successful:	Based on:	Confidence Level:

1. Comparing your top-down and bottom-up analyses, which do you believe has more credibility? Why?

_____

_____

2. If you blend the two estimations, what is your final TAM size? What factors would make the TAM lower than you calculated? What are the factors that would drive the TAM much higher?

_____

_____

_____

STEP 5

Profile the Persona for the Beachhead Market

WHAT IS STEP 5, PROFILE THE PERSONA FOR THE BEACHHEAD MARKET?

Identify one actual real end user in your Beachhead Market who best represents your End User Profile and do a detailed profile on that specific individual.

WHY DO WE DO THIS STEP, AND WHY DO WE DO IT NOW?

The Persona creates great focus in your organization and serves as a touchstone for all decisions going forward.

By the Book: See pages 69–76 of *Disciplined Entrepreneurship* for basic knowledge on this step.
See pages 77–81 of *Disciplined Entrepreneurship* for examples of how different companies and teams have addressed this step.

The Persona clarifies to everyone who is the final arbiter on key decisions on the product.

PROCESS GUIDE

The Persona is very similar to the End User Profile in Step 3, except that it is for one specific individual person and is much more in depth, resulting in an even clearer picture of your target end user.

As a startup, your challenge is to motivate a brand-new team to focus on solving a customer problem/opportunity in a completely new way, and you don't have the resources to let the team spend valuable time squabbling about which direction to go. Logical arguments based on numbers and concepts have their place, but what really pulls the team together and drives them forward is telling a story. Behavioral economists have known for decades that narratives are the most powerful way to motivate people.[1] The Persona is how your startup tells the story of who your customer is and why it matters that you are solving your customer's pain.

As such it is important that the person you choose for your Persona accurately represents your broader End User Profile from Step 3. You should not just take the first willing person or simply choose someone on your team, but rather find the person who is the best you can get. In technical terms, this person sits at the middle of the bell curve and is not an outlier.

The Persona focuses and motivates you and your team to make the right product design decisions as well as all the other decisions needed around the product (e.g., business model, pricing, distribution, messaging) for you to be successful. It takes conversations that would otherwise be abstract debates and makes them concrete, actionable questions. What would the Persona want and find most valuable?

The Persona is a very simple way to keep the focus in the right place. As I always said at my companies, "Keep the main thing the main thing."

The downside of this approach is that no one person can fully represent your target end user in all dimensions, but starting with a focused Persona and adjusting when you think it is leading you astray

---

[1] For more on the power of the narrative, see *Made to Stick* by Chip and Dan Heath and *Why David Sometimes Wins: Leadership, Organization, and Strategy in the California Farm Worker Movement* by Marshall Ganz.

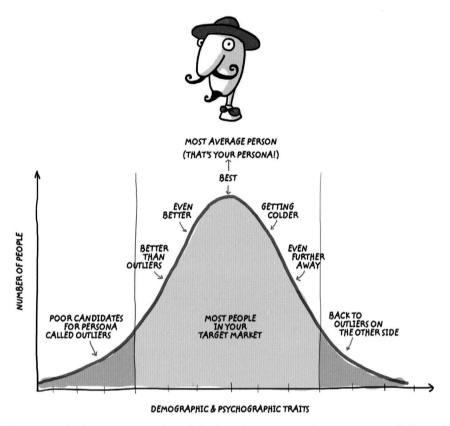

MOST AVERAGE PERSON
(THAT'S YOUR PERSONA!)

BEST

EVEN
BETTER

GETTING
COLDER

BETTER
THAN
OUTLIERS

EVEN
FURTHER
AWAY

NUMBER OF PEOPLE

POOR CANDIDATES
FOR PERSONA
CALLED OUTLIERS

MOST PEOPLE
IN YOUR
TARGET MARKET

BACK TO
OUTLIERS ON
THE OTHER SIDE

DEMOGRAPHIC & PSYCHOGRAPHIC TRAITS

The Persona is the best representative of the broader target market segment in all dimensions.

from your End User Profile is better than not having focus at all. Entrepreneurs have limited resources and time, so you need to create action and a strong, unified team to fight the existing hierarchy of status quo and inertia. You can update the Persona later, especially in Step 9, Identify Your Next 10 Customers, so make your best guess now and keep the process moving because you don't learn without action.

A question I frequently get is whether a member of the founding team can be the Persona. Teams with members who come from the target customer group start the process with deep domain expertise, which is extremely valuable. In fact, this is often the case for many of my classes' most successful teams. If you don't have someone on your team with deep domain expertise in the market you are focused on and who is from the target end user group, you will have to find someone like that and add them to your team early on. When you do, you will be amazed at the insights that person provides.

On the other hand, when you go to the extreme and appoint a member of the founding team as your Persona, you don't know if you've truly found the middle of the bell curve, the person who best exemplifies the target end user group. I have seen it work well, but I've also seen it fail spectacularly. You must be constantly vigilant to analyze whether your Persona is a valid choice, and it can be hard for people to step back and realize they are not the best representation of the broader market. The founder's humility and the strength of the team to hold the founder Persona accountable are key in making it work. In general, I encourage you to use a Persona who is external to your company.

To create the Persona profile, see the two worksheets at the end of this chapter, the General Information on Persona and the Persona Profile for Beachhead Market, which will step you through the information you need to consider in your profile. You may find additional information becomes relevant or some of the fields on the worksheet are not relevant. Make a profile that fits your Persona.

In addition, here are some things to consider when building your Persona:

- It must be a real person. I know this might feel a bit like stalking someone, but marketing researchers have been doing this for years. Keep the details within your team and this can be overcome.

- Make it visual and omnipresent. Your Persona won't motivate people if it's a few paragraphs of text sitting on a dusty shelf. Jeff Bezos at Amazon often insists that an empty chair representing the customer be present at important meetings. What would the customer think? How does your decision create value for that person?

- Specificity is good. Definitely err on the side of too much detail rather than too little, especially at first, but then remove the details that don't add value. If the details explain the mindset of the Persona despite not being directly related to the product, those details are still valuable. However, if they're not directly related to the product and don't provide insight about how the Persona thinks, they are just distractions. Take them out!

- It is very important to do this as a team exercise. Just getting the result and then passing it out to the rest of the team is far less effective than having the team involved as the description of the Persona is being created. If possible, have them involved as well in the discussions and observations with the Persona. The more understanding and buy-in you get from your team on the Persona, the more alignment you will have going forward as a company, and that will make all the difference.

Once you have the Persona, you will start to focus on what you can do to add value for that Persona.

GENERAL EXERCISES TO UNDERSTAND CONCEPT

See the back of the book for answers to these questions.

1. Which advertisement do you think will be more effective to get people to donate money? Why?

   a. According to the World Food Programme, 795 million people in the world do not have enough food to lead a healthy, active life. The vast majority of the world's hungry people live in developing countries, where 12.9 percent of the population is undernourished. Poor nutrition causes 3.1 million deaths in children under 5 years of age each year, roughly 100 million children in developing countries are underweight, 66 million primary school-age children attend classes hungry across the developing world, and the World Food Programme calculates that $3.2 billion is needed per year to reach all 66 million hungry school-age children. Will you donate today for this cause?

   b. Raj Shah is 12 years old and lives in New Delhi. Here's a picture of him and his family. He works in the mornings and evenings to support his mother, Anjali, who is unable to make enough money for her family because she has limited mobility from diabetes, and she also has to take care of her parents. Raj also has to take care of his younger sister, Tanya, who is 7 years old. Raj is trying to go school but having a very hard time because he does not have a nutritious diet, which not only makes him lethargic and unable to focus at school, but can seriously stunt the full development of his brain. Raj has barely eaten anything for 3 weeks now, and certainly nothing healthy, as he is just picking up scraps from what others throw out. There is a good chance that if he does not get a good meal in the next two weeks, he will suffer permanent damage to his brain and body, which will affect his ability to support his extended family. By the way, this is just the story of one child going to school hungry, but there are 66 million of them around the world. Won't you give $50 to help children like Raj to help themselves and their families?

_____

_____

_____

_____

_____

_____

_____

2. What is the bigger challenge for a startup (circle one):

   a. Having enough time to research and figure out the best strategy.

   b. Motivating people to keep making progress so that you can generate momentum and convince others to join you.

3. Persona or Not: When you see a spokesperson for a product, like LeBron James for Kia Motors or Jessica Alba for The Honest Company, are they the Persona? If not, who are they?

_____

_____

_____

_____

_____

_____

_____

_____

_____

WORKSHEETS

General Information on Persona

1	What is the name of your Persona?	
2	Where did you source this person from?	
3	What types of biases are possible with this Persona? (e.g., it is a friend/relative who won't be as honest, the Persona is a potential customer so you might advocate for your product too early instead of staying in inquiry mode)	
4	What will you do to mitigate these biases as you work with the Persona?	
5	What kind of access do you have to the Persona? (Be careful to use their time wisely because they are not as motivated as you by your process.)	
6	What do you see as the strengths of this Persona?	
7	What do you see as the weaknesses of this Persona?	
8	I agree I will revisit this Persona to see if it is the best Persona on an ongoing basis, especially after Step 9, Identify Your Next 10 Customers, and change if a better one is found and willing.	____ Yes (good answer) ____ No ("No" is not a good answer)

Persona Profile for Beachhead Market

<table>
<tr><td colspan="2" align="center">Add a visual image of the Persona here</td></tr>
<tr><td>Name</td><td></td></tr>
<tr><td>Address</td><td></td></tr>
<tr><td>E-mail and phone</td><td></td></tr>
<tr><td>Title (if appropriate)</td><td></td></tr>
<tr><td>If business-to-business (B2B), where they exist in the overall org chart</td><td></td></tr>
<tr><td colspan="2">Demographics:</td></tr>
<tr><td>Gender</td><td></td></tr>
<tr><td>Age</td><td></td></tr>
<tr><td>Income</td><td></td></tr>
<tr><td>Education level</td><td></td></tr>
<tr><td>Education specifics (schools, majors, awards, etc.)</td><td></td></tr>
<tr><td>Employment History (companies, jobs, awards, etc.)</td><td></td></tr>
<tr><td>Marital status</td><td></td></tr>
<tr><td>Kids and other family info</td><td></td></tr>
<tr><td>Ethnicity</td><td></td></tr>
<tr><td>Political affiliations</td><td></td></tr>
<tr><td>Other demographic 1:</td><td></td></tr>
<tr><td>Other demographic 2:</td><td></td></tr>
<tr><td>Other demographic 3:</td><td></td></tr>
<tr><td>Other demographic 4:</td><td></td></tr>
<tr><td colspan="2">Psychographics:</td></tr>
<tr><td>Why do they do this job or live the life they do?</td><td></td></tr>
</table>

Hobbies	
Heroes	
Aspirations in life	
Fears in life	
Personality traits	
Interesting habits	
Other psychographic 1:	
Other psychographic 2:	
Other psychographic 3:	
Other psychographic 4:	

Proxy Products (which products have the highest correlation with your Persona)	
Is there a product or products that the Persona needs to have in order to get benefit from yours?	
Are there products the Persona uses that embody the psychographics and demographics from the end user profile?	
Any other unusual or interesting products of note that the Persona has?	

Watering Holes (real or virtual places where the Persona interacts with others like him or her):	
Favorite sources for news (e.g., which newspapers, TV shows, websites, blogs)	
Places where Persona congregates with other similar people	
Associations Persona belongs to and the importance of each	
Where does the Persona go for expert advice and/or to get questions answered?	

Day in the Life (describe a day in the life of the end user and what is going on in this person's head):	
What are the typical tasks the Persona does each day, with the amount of time associated with each?	
Which of these typical tasks are habits?	
Which require the most effort?	
Which does the Persona enjoy?	
Which does the Persona not enjoy?	
What makes it a good day for the Persona?	
What makes it a bad day?	
Who is the Persona trying to please the most?	
What is the top priority of the person/people the Persona is trying to please?	

Priorities:	
Priorities (what are your Persona's priorities—focus first on biggest fears, then biggest motivations— and assign a weighting to each so that it adds up to 100)	1. _____ Weighting: _____ 2. _____ Weighting: _____ 3. _____ Weighting: _____ 4. _____ Weighting: _____ 5. _____ Weighting: _____
	Now, revisit the General Information worksheet and update as needed, especially for items 3, 4, 6, and 7.

Note: These worksheets are meant to guide you but not constrain you. The Persona should paint a rich picture and convey important information about your target market, so feel free to customize this worksheet as appropriate.

ADVANCED TOPIC: PERSONA PROFILES FOR MULTISIDED END USER MARKET

How do you build a Persona profile when you have multiple types of end users for your startup, such as with the increasingly common platforms being built today? The fundamental concept is the same, designating one Persona for each type of end user, but the Persona profiles must be coordinated and consistent with each other.

Awa Kone, Jeronimo van Schendel, Lisa Tacoronte, and Benedita Sampaio e Mello took my class at MIT and worked on a project to create a platform, dubbed "BuildLine," to help designers, contractors, and suppliers to better collaborate when turning ideas into tangible products by making relevant peer connections and facilitating the project management process.

While the team had some significant domain expertise in this field, they chose wisely to make the Personas people other than themselves. You will see excellent Personas for all three sides of the proposed new venture (but not perfect, as they never are, especially for a one-semester course where so much has to be covered).

You'll notice how they handled and coordinated all three sides of the end user market. I really like the detail summarized in one slide for each Persona, so you get a rich understanding of each Persona and can quickly determine what is most important to each, which is highly beneficial when you have to make decisions keeping three Personas in mind instead of just one.

I would have liked to see more on product proxies and watering holes, and at times I felt like their profiles veered more toward advocacy for the product as opposed to focusing solely on understanding who the Personas are, but all in all, they did a tremendous job!

First, an overview of the players in BuildLine:

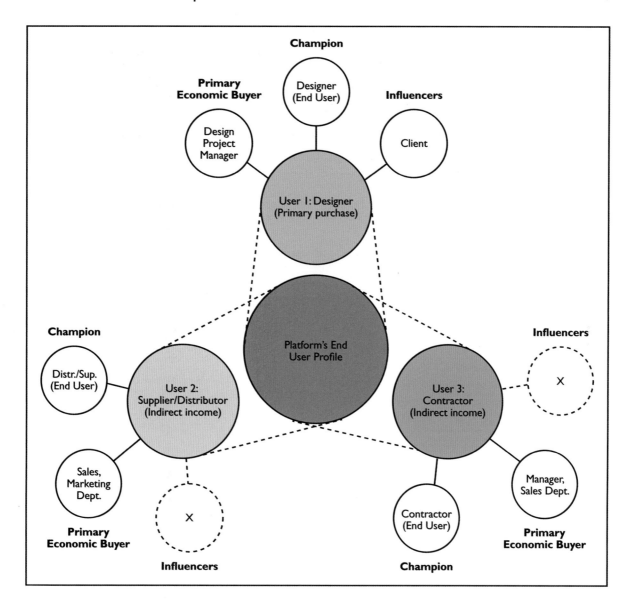

Then, the three Personas for BuildLine:

PERSONA 1/3

John Smith
New York City Architect

ESSENTIALS

Age: 41
Family: Wife and 2 kids
Originally from outside the United States.

EDUCATION & CURRENT POSITION

School and Degree: Master's in Architecture from an architecture or technology school (name of school omitted for this workbook).

Years in industry: 4-15 years.

Title: Chief Architect and Co-founder of his own boutique firm.

Income: Amount of office profit omitted for this workbook.

Key responsibilities: manage project, stakeholders, lead designer and visionary, source and approve contractors & suppliers

Photograph of him goes here
(omitted for this workbook)

Demographics, facts + Psychographics

◄———————————►

ONE WEEK WITH HIM

Working hours: ~10-12 hours per day on average. Typical day: May begin at 6 or 8am and end at 6 or 8pm.

Starts with the latest architectural news in publications, blogs, and magazines. Answers emails, reviews new proposals and current project statuses, attends morning team update meetings with senior associates. In the afternoon he attends client meetings and throughout the day he works on sketches, software drawings, fields phone calls, checks in on consultants, contractors and suppliers for progress.

Summary of typical weekly objectives/tasks:

Review and approve proposals.

Lead sketches and virtual drawings for the client

Make decisions in existing projects to move through phases.

Check in with key stakeholders and progress of materials and projects.

And his priorities are:

Professional	Personal
Quality designs within budget and time	Family. Wife and kids.
Recognition in industry and academia (nice projects).	Intellectually keeping abreast.
His staff	Health and wellbeing

HIS OFFICE

Successful or award-winning architectural firm. Small to medium size with 5-20 employees ranging from principals to designers and about 3-4 levels of hierarchy. Clients range from museums to airports, art galleries, and other companies for redesign of their offices.

IN THE MIRROR... WHAT HE VALUES

He believes his work happens at the cross-section of architecture, academia and the arts. He values creativity, intellect, innovation, and artistic originality. He appreciates simplicity and clean lines. Functionally elegant with a non-obtrusive form. He also values efficiency, hard work, and passion in the design he produces.

HIS DREAMS

Become a leading voice in the architectural field. He hopes to make it into renowned textbooks as gold standards for architectural design of his time. He would like his firm to remain as a boutique business but be able to increase its income at little cost. On a personal level, he loves his children, and wants them to likewise succeed artistically and intellectually.

ALSO FEARS AND FRUSTRATIONS...

Lack of stable work for his firm and not being able to provide for staff and family.

Frustrated with the increasing cost of and time spent finding and securing contractors and suppliers, and time spent negotiating budget and time constraints with clients.

He fears erosion of margins on his projects as clients begin negotiating harder on his fees.

Frustrated with the lack of trust and quality of his collaborators, risking his own reputation.

PERSONA 2/3

Jane Frank
New York City Architect

ESSENTIALS

Age: 35
Family: Recently married. One young kid.
Originally from NYC.

EDUCATION & CURRENT POSITION

School/major, current position, and salary omitted for this worksheet.

HER OFFICE

Works in the brand's flagship store. Designers and clients from all over the city come to see their products. She manages the Bathroom section, where there are two other employees.

She receives the people and presents the collection, then she derives them to others, who repeat over and over the characteristics of each variant. People come between one and four times before deciding about a product.

She needs to push for sales, and keep up with trends.

ONE WEEK WITH HER

Typical day: (10am to 8pm, Mon-Sat) 50% of time at her desk, 50% speaking to clients.

Events outside the routine: items renovation, reorganizing the product exhibition, organizing sales campaigns. A lot of fairs...

Typical weekly objectives: sell, sell, sell. Manage stock.

Photograph of her goes here
(omitted for this workbook)

Demographics, facts + Psychographics

⟵⟶

And her priorities are:

Professional | Personal

Sell, sell, sell. Capture clients, if they are not individuals, better. | Family and friends.

Maintain high presence in the field's events. | Image, relation with the right people, a door to her dreams.

Keep up with stock and showroom. | Income.

IN THE MIRROR... WHAT SHE VALUES

She sees herself as someone with a sort of objective sense of taste, but more than anything with knowledge of what's next in the decoration field, so she can tell you what to use, what to buy, depending on who you are.

As a person, she is completely of the social kind, really open and dynamic always interested in consuming trends and up to date, more than in deeply understanding any of them.

HER DREAMS AND WATERING HOLES

Deep in her heart, she would love to apply that taste sense to open her own store or interior design studio, for the moment this paycheck seems logical, and she can also do that on the side, until one day...

Anyway, that dream does not prevent her from sleeping. This aspect is important, but as much as having fun, having a family and keeping in contact with trends.

Waterholes are generally the place where she mixes with admired people: design exhibitions, show room openings, fairs, where she works, and any related ones.

ALSO FEARS AND FRUSTRATIONS...

This job is quite active, but not as creative as she can be. Will staying here mean renouncing or losing some of her capacities? And on the other hand, she cannot quit like that... Any other design option is risky.

Family and friends are very important, anything that contradicts that seems inappropriate.

Finally, her environment is quite a high-end one. She fears not keeping up with the page in that job.

PERSONA 3/3

Peter MacDonald
New York State Contractor

ESSENTIALS

Age: 45
Family: Wife and 2 kids (ages omitted for this workbook.
Originally from upstate New York.

EDUCATION & CURRENT POSITION

School/major, current position, and salary omitted for this worksheet.

HIS OFFICE

His office is half in the construction fields, half in the company headquarters. He is pretty much on the phone every day at every moment, managing people and fighting to keep risk under its limits. He decides everything—the sales, the relationships, the subcontractors...

He has three employees who are direct collaborators, who can strongly influence his decisions: the crew and materials coordinator, the 2nd chief engineer, and the budget manager. The rest are interpreting drawings, sourcing materials and people, and bidding constantly.

ONE WEEK WITH HIM

Construction works starts early (7am) in the morning, and can go until very late. Usually has several important field visits per day. He moves in a pick-up from building sites to clients' offices, to product factories, etc.

Events outside the routine: every day there is one issue to solve. But bidding is the most important moment, where everything needs to be played at one time.

Photograph of him goes here
(omitted for this workbook)

Demographics, facts + Psychographics

← →

And his priorities are:

Professional | Personal

Getting new works. Winning bids. | Family. Wife and kids.

Finding and managing the right people (subcontractors). | Wealth. Not excessive, but to maintain a fairly good life.

Reducing risk as much as possible. | Doing interesting work.

IN THE MIRROR... WHAT HE VALUES

He is a "doer" with a fairly high amount of technical expertise. He is a simple person, with a certain taste for craftmanship. He can find a point of connection with designers through it, although he does not really understand what's the point on worrying so much for minor or overcomplicated things. Overall he has a sense of practicality, which he puts on top of every decision and work he makes.

Although he likes his work and he needs it to feel alive, he is not extremely attached to what he does, apart from the sense of pride of well-done work.

His family is the most important thing.

HIS DREAMS!!!

Making his company grow. Working in bigger and bigger challenges.

Finding works that are different to what everybody does.

Becoming a recognized working expert in some particular field of construction.

A house for vacations in a beautiful countryside landscape. And a future for his family.

ALSO FEARS AND FRUSTRATIONS...

Professionally, he fears three types of risk:

• Risk for underpricing a work in a bid—losing money.

• Risk for technical problems which imply overexpenses.

• Risk for his or his workers' health. In the construction field, accidents can happen very easily.

STEP 6

Full Life Cycle Use Case

WHAT IS STEP 6, FULL LIFE CYCLE USE CASE?

Understand and describe the full context of how your product will fit into your Persona's workflow. This is the customer's perspective.

WHY DO WE DO THIS STEP, AND WHY DO WE DO IT NOW?

The Full Life Cycle Use Case provides valuable information for future steps and also helps the team understand potential barriers to adoption from a sales perspective. Now that you have the Persona, you can do a lot of the primary market research required to complete this step, but your output will still be just a first draft because you won't have enough information to define this step completely.

By the Book: See pages 83–86 of *Disciplined Entrepreneurship* for basic knowledge on this step.
See pages 86–90 of *Disciplined Entrepreneurship* for examples of how different companies and teams have addressed this step.

Without understanding the Full Life Cycle Use Case, your product will have no context and generate little to no value.

PROCESS GUIDE

Observe not just what you are doing in this step, but what you are not doing. Now that you have a Persona, shouldn't you simply ask what that person thinks about your product idea? No! You do not have nearly enough information to start advocating for the customer to buy your product.

How about starting to design your product? That time is coming. In the next step, you'll start outlining the specifics of your product, but first, you need to focus on the overall context your product will fit into. High-quality products often fail because too much time is focused on the technology or the features, and too little time on how the end users would integrate the new product into how they currently go about their lives. You'll explore the latter in the Full Life Cycle Use Case.

As with all of these steps, your goal is to spend enough time, effort, and thought to get a useful first draft, but you will continually update this information as you move to future steps, especially Step 13, Map the Process to Acquire a Paying Customer. You also want to keep using primary market research to fill out this information, rather than guessing or extrapolating based on existing research or intuition. With a grounding in primary market research, you'll end up with a valuable set of information that will prove a competitive advantage—don't give away this information!

To map out the Full Life Cycle Use Case, first use the Sketch of How the End User Currently Solves the Problem (or Doesn't) worksheet to sketch out a visual diagram or flowchart showing how customers currently attempt to solve their pain, or what processes result in their customer pain. Without understanding customers' current workflow, you will have a hard time getting your new product in their hands, because people don't like to change how they go about things, especially if they are satisfied with their current workflow.

Next, you will use the Full Life Cycle Use Case worksheet to map out everything related to the end user's discovery, acquisition, and use of your product. Here is an overview of the 10 stages of the Full Life Cycle Use Case, updated from the original definition in *Disciplined Entrepreneurship*.

10 Stages of Full Life Cycle Use Case

For each stage in the cycle, explain who will be involved in that step, when and where the step occurs, and how it happens, as well as other detail that seems relevant. Entries in the worksheet will have dramatically different complexity. For business-to-consumer (B2C) companies, the entries maybe very simple, even trivial, but for business-to-business (B2B), the answers will likely be much more complex in certain areas.

How the end user actually uses your product will likely be the most complex part to describe. Give some brief bullet points on this worksheet, and then use the Sketch of How End User Will Use Your Product worksheet to provide a visual overview with diagrams, flowcharts, and pictures.

The result of this step will be a body of information about the end user's interaction with the product so that your team is on the same page before starting to design the product itself. If the team is not in alignment on the workflow sketched out here, individual team members will pull the product in different directions, reducing the clarity you'll have around whether your product is effective at solving the end user's customer pain.

GENERAL EXERCISES TO UNDERSTAND CONCEPT

See the back of the book for answers to some of these questions.

1. As of June 2016, Android users were able to choose between 2.2 million apps, and Apple's App Store had 2 million available apps. Yet very few of them have been successful. Why do most mobile phone apps fail to become economically interesting or viable? (Circle one)

   a. They don't have the right functionality.

   b. People don't know about the app.

2. Take two products that you use a lot, one in your personal life and one in your business life. In less than one hour, using intuition and secondary sources if needed, try to map the Full Life Cycle Use Case for each product using a copy of the Full Life Cycle Use Case worksheet.

WORKSHEETS

Sketch of How the End User Currently Solves The Problem (or Doesn't)

Full Life Cycle Use Case Worksheet

Stage #	1	2	3	4	5	6	7	8	9	10
Action	*How do they determine need, and what is their catalyst to take action?*	*How do they find out about their options?*	*How do they analyze their options?*	*How do they acquire your product?*	*How do they pay for your product?*	*How do they install or set up your product?*	*How do they use and get value out of your product?*	*How do they determine the value they gain from your product?*	*How do they buy more of your product?*	*How do they tell others about your product?*
Who is involved										
When										
Where										
How										
Misc.										

Sketch of How the End User Will Use Your Product

Reflection on Full Life Cycle Use Case

1. Looking at these worksheets now, where do you see the gaps in your understanding?

_____

_____

2. How do you intend to fill those knowledge gaps?

_____

_____

3. Which stages of the Full Life Cycle Use Case are you most concerned about as posing risks to the adoption of your new solution?

_____

_____

    You have completed your first draft of the Full Life Cycle Use Case! You are probably at least a bit uncomfortable with some aspects of it, and that's understandable; plan to circle back to it as you complete additional steps and gain more understanding. But let's keep moving forward and start to define what your product would be within this overall context.

STEP 7

High-Level Product Specification

WHAT IS STEP 7, HIGH-LEVEL PRODUCT SPECIFICATION?

Create a visual description of the product and make a simple draft of a brochure.

WHY DO WE DO THIS STEP, AND WHY DO WE DO IT NOW?

You need to make sure that all your team has a common agreement on what the product is. You have likely had an idea from the beginning of what your product will be. Now that you know who the customer is and in what context that person will use your product, you can intelligently start the process of defining your product.

By the Book: See pages 91–94 of *Disciplined Entrepreneurship* for basic knowledge on this step. See pages 94–101 of *Disciplined Entrepreneurship* for examples of how different companies and teams have addressed this step.

As you translate your idea into a product spec, you'll find out whether your team is on the same page!

PROCESS GUIDE

"Finally," you say, "now we can start to talk about the product!" Yes, now is the time. Why did I wait so long? Simple: I wanted you to stay open minded. It was important that you be in full "inquiry mode" and not be in "advocacy mode."[1] Staying in inquiry mode significantly increases the odds that you will design a product your target customer loves and gets optimal value from.

In this step, you will build a High-Level Product Specification and ultimately a first draft brochure (which can be physical and/or digital, but the concept and content is essentially the same). This achieves the following important objectives:

1. Drives a common understanding, on the team and beyond, of what product the company is thinking of producing. It is more common than not where team members have different ideas of what product they are aspiring to develop. This process forces explicit alignment and often surprises the team to see the level of misalignment they had before the exercise.

2. Creates a focus on benefits rather than features and functions. Teams, especially technical teams, often start to get into feature wars with competitors and lose focus on the customer,

---

[1] I talked in more depth about this in the *TechCrunch* article of March 1, 2014, titled "Our Dangerous Obsession with the MVP;" see https://techcrunch.com/2014/03/01/our-dangerous-obsession-with-the-mvp/.

who only sees the benefits (or lack thereof) that a feature provides. This exercise will keep the emphasis on benefits.

3. Begins the process of prioritizing which benefits are more important than others. You'll focus not just your messaging but also the product design/development and business model/pricing.

4. Gives you something concrete to discuss and iterate on with the Persona (and later, other customers) while staying in "inquiry mode." It is very easy to change a brochure as opposed to a prototype, because brochures don't take much time to develop, so you're much less invested and attached to it than a prototype. Don't let the "IKEA effect" blind you to what the customer really wants.[2]

Start by completing the Visual Representation of Product worksheet, keeping in mind the following attributes of an effective High-Level Product Specification:

1. **Visual**: If it is hardware, this is easy and surprisingly clarifying. For software, use a series of simulated screenshots to form a storyboard that shows how someone would use the product.

2. **Focus on benefits**: Focus on the benefits and not the technology or functionality. In particular, focus on the benefits that are related to the Persona's top three priorities, with special focus on the top priority. Benefits are what matter to a savvy customer. Be clear on the value proposition this product has for the end user.

3. **High level**: Don't include too much detail! Just enough to show high-level functionality that will drive the benefits.

4. **Hits the spot**: Make sure the product specification resonates deeply with the Persona and other customers in the target End User Profile group. Conversely, don't be influenced by people outside your Beachhead Market, because they won't help you achieve a dominant market share in your beachhead.

5. **Flexible**: Make sure your product specification builds in the ability to iterate with the Persona about key features, functions, and benefits. Some people make multiple versions and show them side by side to the Persona. Listen to what the Persona says, and always be willing to change what you have done. A wise man once said, "Listening is the willingness to change." Don't ignore your Persona's feedback just because you think the brochure is great.

Next, complete the Product Alignment with Persona worksheet. Does your high-level specification line up with your Persona's key priorities? Is it ready for review with your Persona? And once it is, what feedback does your Persona provide, and how will you revise the specification in response?

Remember that the Persona's job is not to design the product for you, but to provide feedback on whether the benefits are useful. And as I cover in Step 23, Show That "The Dogs Will Eat the Dog Food," the ultimate test will come later, when it comes time for your customers to pay for your product.

As part of this step, you should also strongly consider creating a product brochure. (I require it in my classes.) Because a brochure can add distractions and unnecessary complications, I have saved discussion of a brochure for the Advanced Topics section at the end of this chapter.

---

[2] "IKEA Effect: When Labor Leads to Love," *Harvard Business* Review working paper, http://www.hbs.edu/faculty/Publication%20 Files/11-091.pdf.

GENERAL EXERCISES TO UNDERSTAND CONCEPT

See the back of the book for answers to some of these questions.

1. **Examples:** Pick three products you use a lot and find a high-level product description/brochure (not the technical specifications) for each one. You may find it on the product section of the website of the company that makes the product. If you find the technical specifications, compare that document with the high-level product description to observe the differences. For each product's high-level description, consider the following questions:

	Product 1= ___	Product 2= ___	Product 3= ___
What customer segment are they targeting?			
What is the primary benefit to that group?			
Is the primary benefit in alignment with the features and function?			
What is unique about the product? Is it clear from the high-level description?			
What did you like about it?			
What didn't you like about it?			

2. **Feature–function–benefit:** A new mobile phone is launched that has an advanced fingerprint reader security system. Identify which of the following is the feature, the function, and the benefit:

   a. Better security for the phone allows important data and information to be stored with peace of mind, which improves your productivity. This is a _____.

   b. Patented active capacitance sensing technology. This is a _____.

   c. Fingerprint recognition is integrated into the phone. This is a _____.

3. **Apply to examples:** Now, for the three products you chose in question 1, identify what their features, functions, and benefits are:

	Product 1= ___	Product 2= ___	Product 3= ___
Features:			
Functions:			
Benefits:			

WORKSHEETS

Visual Representation of Product

In the space below (use more sheets if need be, but keep it to no more than three sheets), build a visual representation of your product and how it works. Annotate your drawings, but do not burden them with too much detail.

Product Alignment with Persona

	How will you deliver a new level of value with respect to this priority?	What features address this priority?	What functions address this priority?	What benefits address this priority?
Persona's #1 Priority: _____				
Persona's #2 Priority: _____				
Persona's #3 Priority: _____				

Ready for Action?

1. Is the High-Level Product Specification ready to review with your Persona? (Circle "Yes" or "No" below.)

   Yes

   No

2. Have you done so? What feedback did the Persona provide?

   _____

   _____

3. Have you iterated at least once based on the Persona's feedback? What changes did you make in response to the Persona's feedback? (Hopefully, you will iterate with the Persona more than once.)

   _____

   _____

4. Has the Persona concluded that the High-Level Product Specification is interesting and satisfies the Persona's priorities? (Circle "Yes" or "No" below.)

   Yes

   No

ADVANCED TOPIC: HIGH-LEVEL PRODUCT BROCHURE

Once you have iterated on your High-Level Product Specification, you may want to build a trifold brochure that more clearly outlines the benefits your product provides. Some people will wait to make a brochure until they have iterated the specification with other customers in Step 9, Identify Your Next 10 Customers, but others find a brochure useful at this stage.

A good brochure should have the following items:

1. First draft of company name and tagline.

2. Name of product and tagline.

3. Image or picture of product so it is clear what it is.

4. Clearly identified benefits aligned with the Persona's #1 priority (don't be subtle—it should come out in the taglines and even maybe even the name of your product).

5. Two additional benefits (if appropriate), aligned with the second and third priorities of the Persona, that don't dilute the impact of the first benefit.

6. Provide a sense of the magnitude of the benefit to be expected by the end user. Use your work from Step 6, Full Life Cycle Use Case.

7. Some other information might be relevant, but always be diligent about not diluting your main message—if you say too much, you say nothing in particular.

8. Have a clear call to action.

9. Everything should be fully aligned with the customer's priorities and will resonate with the customer in all elements (e.g., names, taglines, pictures, benefits emphasized, fonts, colors, word choice, language, references, call to action).

There are great individuals and agencies you can hire to design brochures, and you're not expected to become an expert in design. But you want to think through the content and make sure it is compelling and addresses the Persona's priorities. That way, if you choose to delegate or outsource the design, you can give them good direction and not settle for an inferior brochure.

Ultimately, the brochure is the most commonly and widely given elevator pitch about your product because it can be done when you are not in the room and even when you are sleeping. It makes consistent messaging possible and scalable, so don't just downplay it as "marketing hype." It really matters.

You also have to back it up with a great product, but that is coming. First, you have to make sure you are building the right product for your customer, and this process really helps to communicate that to all sides.

STEP 8

Quantify the Value Proposition

WHAT IS STEP 8, QUANTIFY THE VALUE PROPOSITION?

In as concrete and concise a way as possible, summarize the value your product will create for the targeted end user.

WHY DO WE DO THIS STEP, AND WHY DO WE DO IT NOW?

Customers will be much more likely to buy your product if the value it provides lines up with their highest priorities. Now that you have defined the Persona's priorities, and you have a Full Life Cycle Use Case and High-Level Product Specification, quantifying your product's value proposition is the missing step to validate that you are headed in the right direction and that your product is in line with the customer's needs.

By the Book: See pages 103–106 of *Disciplined Entrepreneurship* for basic knowledge on this step. See pages 106–110 of *Disciplined Entrepreneurship* for examples of how different companies and teams have addressed this step.

The Quantified Value Proposition makes crystal clear what benefits you bring to the customer.

PROCESS GUIDE

Start by taking your Persona's #1 priority from the Persona Profile worksheet. Talk with the Persona about how to measure that priority quantitatively, and what units to measure it in. For instance, if your Persona's top priority is saving money, then your value proposition will likely be expressed as dollars, or dollars per time period (such as dollars saved over the course of a year). If it is reliability, your measurement might be percentage rate of failure, errors per thousand products, downtime per month, or a similar measurement.

Next, take that quantitative measurement and map out how the Persona currently operates in the "as-is state." Interview the Persona to get this information, and use the Persona's own words when describing the as-is state. Use the space later on in this chapter to take notes about how the Persona describes the as-is state. Then, use the top half of the Quantified Value Proposition worksheet to visually break it down into concrete steps or stages.

For instance, if your product reduces time to market for the Persona's products, such as in the SensAble example in *Disciplined Entrepreneurship* (pages 106–108), map out each stage of the process by which a product is produced. In the SensAble example for developing a new toy, there were four discrete processes: ideation, tech package design, a "looks like/works like" testing period, and a commercialization process. Since they are measuring their priority as time to market, the as-is state would show how long, in days, each of the four processes takes.

Once you have mapped out the as-is state, review it with the Persona to make sure you clearly understand how things currently stand, and the Persona agrees with the terminology and the data. If the Persona does not understand the as-is state, you will have trouble demonstrating how your product can benefit the Persona.

Next, define the possible state in the same terms as you just did for the as-is state with your proposed new product. Explicitly show how your proposed product will better satisfy the Persona's #1 priority in detail. Express the possible state by using the same units with which you measured the Persona's top priority.

Calculating the possible state will be a challenge because you have only just begun to settle on what the product will be. But this exercise will help you better understand what product your customer wants you to build.

A few tips:

- Don't overpromise the benefit your product will provide in the possible state. You want to "underpromise" and "overdeliver" because as a new startup, you have little to no credibility, so all you have are your promises. You do not want your customer to lose trust in what you say or for competitors to seize on your every misstep and point out your flaws. And in a startup, rarely do things go as planned, so you want some buffer for slippages and surprises. If your Persona is not excited by your conservative value proposition and is only excited by a more aggressive set of promises, that should signal danger to you.

- Sometimes, the Persona has multiple top priorities that are intertwined. See in *Disciplined Entrepreneurship* the example for InTouch, where the Persona, a pregnant mother-to-be, wanted reassurance that her fetus was healthy and wanted to establish intimacy with her unborn child. The InTouch product was meant to address both priorities, as the priorities were similar enough in theme that one product could easily satisfy both priorities without losing clarity on the product's mission.

GENERAL EXERCISES TO UNDERSTAND CONCEPT

1. **Examples:** For successful products with savvy product marketers, their alignment with the customer's #1 priority is evident in their taglines and advertisements, and is repeated over and over again until their target customer can hear it in their sleep. If I say "Volvo" to an audience and ask them what word comes to mind, they immediately say "safety." That association completely resonates with Volvo's target market of upper-middle-class mothers. If I say "Verizon," the word that comes up, not by accident but by a multimillion-dollar marketing campaign, is "reliability," which is exactly what business professionals, Verizon's target customer, want to hear. In both cases, the companies use a combination of anecdotes and data to back up their claims. Pick a product you are passionate about and explore its marketing materials. Is it clear what its value proposition is to you? Does the company present the value proposition quantitatively? Using what units? How effectively does the company get its value proposition across? How effective is it for you based on your priorities? What would you find more compelling?

WORKSHEETS

Axis to Measure Value Proposition

1. What is the Persona's #1 priority?

_____

2. What units should it be measured in?

_____

Persona's General Verbal Description of the "As Is" State and the Opportunities for Improvement

_____

_____

_____

_____

_____

_____

_____

_____

_____

_____

Persona's General Verbal Description of the "Possible" State and the Opportunities for Improvement

_____

_____

_____

_____

_____

_____

_____

_____

_____

_____

Visual One-Page Summary of Quantified Value Proposition

On the page below, draw diagrams that represent the "as is" state and "possible" state, and summarize the benefits to the customer.

Quantified Value Proposition

"As is" State

Result in "As Is":
_____
_____
_____
_____

#1 Priority of Persona: _____

"Possible" State

Result in "Possible":
_____
_____

Summary of Benefits:
_____
_____

Reason for Benefits:
_____
_____

At this stage in the process, you should now be feeling pretty good. You know who your customer is, and you have an overview of what product you'd like to build and what value it will deliver. You have made great progress, but you will need to refine all of this a great deal more to develop a go-to-market strategy and build and launch your product. Regardless, completing this step is still an important milestone—congratulations!

STEP 9

Identify Your Next 10 Customers

WHAT IS STEP 9, IDENTIFY YOUR NEXT 10 CUSTOMERS?

Create a list of the next 10 end users after the Persona who closely fit the End User Profile. Engage them in a dialogue on your plans and validate or invalidate what you have done so far.

WHY DO WE DO THIS STEP, AND WHY DO WE DO IT NOW?

Identifying and speaking with 10 additional end users in detail at this point with regard to the work you have done will provide you with extremely valuable data points to refine the work you have done in each step, and will validate or invalidate many of the assumptions you have made. By the end of this step, you should have a much-improved End User Profile, Beachhead Market, Total Addressable Market (TAM) size, Full Life Cycle Use Case, High-Level Product Specification, and Quantified Value Proposition, and either you will have greater confidence in your selection of Persona or you will have changed your selection. Doing a first pass on all of these steps was necessary to have productive conversations with the additional end users you will interact with in this step.

By the Book: See pages 113–117 of *Disciplined Entrepreneurship* for basic knowledge on this step. See pages 117–119 of *Disciplined Entrepreneurship* for examples of how different companies and teams have addressed this step.

Finding 10 customers whose traits are the same as the Persona gives you crucial information to validate that you are headed in the right direction.

PROCESS GUIDE

The primary market research involved in contacting 10 additional end users and conversing with them about their customer pain will quickly refine and validate or invalidate the work you have done so far.

Start by identifying what you want to gain from talking with additional end users. What hypotheses about your work thus far are you looking to validate during this step? Use the second half of the Lessons Learned worksheet at the end of this chapter to list the main hypotheses you will test before engaging potential customers. Make sure that the conversations you have with end users focus on these hypotheses.

Next, make a list of potential end users to contact. You will need to list more than 10 people since you might not be able to contact or engage with some of the people on your list. Use the List of Potential Contacts worksheet to record their information, including where you found out about them ("source") and, to the best of your knowledge, how closely they match the characteristics of your Persona and End User Profile. You should update this after each conversation.

It is important that you are able to find a truly homogeneous market (i.e., same product, same sales process, and strong word of mouth) in your Next 10 Customers. A common mistake startups make is pretending they have a homogeneous market when they don't. Don't delude yourself—be intellectually honest! Don't settle for the first 10 people whom you can convince to talk to you. You need a homogeneous group of people who are very similar to your Persona.

You also don't want to talk to people who are not the end user. While the person who decides to buy the product (the economic buyer) is important, as well as key decision makers and influencers, talking to them will not help you solve the end user's customer pain, and therefore the product you design will not be readily adopted.

As you start to talk with the people on your list, take notes about each contact, using the Notes from Conversation with Potential End User worksheet as a guide. Use a new worksheet for each conversation. Pay close attention to the following categories to make sure you have end users who truly match your criteria:

- Demographics
- Psychographics

- Overall Profile
- Full Life Cycle Use Case
- Quantified Value Proposition

At the end of the conversation, if the end user seems like a good fit, ask if they would be willing to provide a nonbinding letter of intent to purchase the product. As I remind you in *Disciplined Entrepreneurship*, you are still in inquiry mode, so suddenly asking, "Will you provide a letter of intent?" may well be off-putting. Instead, ask more softly and generally, "If a company were to offer this product, would you make a commitment to purchase it?"

After each conversation, jot down notes about whether the potential end user validated or invalidated any of your hypotheses. Also think about whether the end user might be a better Persona than your current Persona. There is nothing wrong with changing your Persona! Having an even slightly better Persona in terms of fit and/or accessibility to your team will pay enormous dividends going forward.

Once you have contacted 10 individuals who are good fits for your End User Profile, fill out the Summary of Next 10 Customers worksheet with summary information about each person you contacted. You want to make sure that when you put all 10 people in the same table, the information is consistent between them—they all are similar enough that they can be considered part of the same market—and that there was a strong amount of interest in purchasing your product across the board. If either of these two areas is weak, you may need to reassess some fundamental concepts in the work you have done so far.

Finally, complete the Lessons Learned worksheet by going back and filling out the first half with an explanation of the process you used to source these potential end users and the conclusions you reached about your hypotheses as a result of your discussions. This table will help you identify which steps you should consider revising. While you should be continually assessing your work at all times during this process, the table will help you clearly identify trouble spots that must be addressed before continuing.

GENERAL EXERCISES TO UNDERSTAND CONCEPT

See the back of the book for answers to these questions.

1. **Interpreting the results of the List of Next 10 Customers:** Two teams have put together their summaries of their Next 10 Customers after doing lots of primary market research. What conclusions can you reach about the strength of each team's product–market fit? What questions do you have for them?

   a. **Team 1:** Lots of interest (see table on next page)

Summary of Next 10 Customers: Team 1

	Fit					Engagement		
#	Demo-graphic	Psycho-graphic	Use Case	Value Prop	Overall	Contacted	Level of Interest— LOI?	Source
1	A	A	A	A	A	YES	A	From Persona
2	B	B	C	B	B	YES	A	School Friend
3	C	B	B	B	B	YES	A	Neighbor
4	C	A	B	A	B	YES	A	From Persona
5	B	B	B	A	B	YES	A	Family friend
6	B	B	B	B	B	YES	A	Alumni Database
7	B	B	B	B	B	YES	A	Classmate
8	C	A	B	B	B	YES	A	Classmate
9	C	B	B	B	B	YES	A/B	Friend of a Friend
10	C	C	C	B	B/C	YES	A/B	From Persona

Legend:

Fit: A = Excellent, B = Medium, C = Poor

Level of Interest: A = Signed a letter of intent, B = unwilling to sign letter of intent, C = refuses to buy the product "Use Case" means that the Full Life Cycle Use Case resonated with how the end user operates. "Value Prop" means the benefit your product delivers is in line with that end user's top priority.

b. **Team 2**: Discipline on fit but not as much interest

Summary of Next 10 Customers: Team 2

	Fit					Engagement		
#	Demo-graphic	Psycho-graphic	Use Case	Value Prop	Overall	Contacted	Level of Interest— LOI?	Source
1	A	A	A	A	A	YES	A+ (NEEDS IT NOW)	From Industry Group
2	A	A	A	A	A	YES	A	From Persona
3	B	A	A	A	A	YES	A	Cold Call /E-mail
4	A	A	A	A	A	YES	A	From Industry Group
5	B	A	A	A	A	YES	Needs to Know More but Interested	Cold Call /E-mail
6	A	A	A	A	A	Early Stages	Needs to Know More but Interested	From Industry Group
7	A	A	A	A	A	Early Stages	Needs to Know More but Interested	From Persona
8	B	A	A	A	A	Early Stages	Needs to Know More but Interested	From Industry Group
9	A	A	A	A	A	Not Yet	Needs to Know More but Interested	From Industry Group
10	A	A	A	A	A	Not Yet	?	From Industry Group

Conclusions and questions for Team 1:

_____

_____

_____

_____

_____

_____

_____

_____

_____

Conclusions and questions for Team 2:

_____

_____

_____

_____

_____

_____

_____

_____

_____

Which team seems to have stronger product–market fit?

_____

_____

_____

_____

_____

_____

_____

_____

_____

WORKSHEETS

List of Potential Contacts

Name	Title	Email/Phone	Source	How closely do they match the Persona/end user profile?

Name	Title	Email/Phone	Source	How closely do they match the Persona/end user profile?

Summary of Next 10 Customers

#	General Info				Fit						Engagement		
	Customer Name	Relevant Info	Title	E-mail/ Phone	Demo- graphic	Psycho- graphic	Use Case	Value Prop	Overall	Contacted	Level of Interest—Letter of Intent?	Source
1												
2												
3												
4												
5												
6												
7												
8												
9												
10												

Note 1: Like with other worksheets, this is meant to give some structure, but it can and should be customized as appropriate for your situation.

Note 2: Relevant Info is other relevant info that is not captured elsewhere, such as "Total Megawatts Installed" for the Methane Capture example from *Disciplined Entrepreneurship*.

Notes from Conversation with Potential End User

Make a copy of this worksheet for each end user you talk to.

Demographics (Be sure to determine which are relevant for your situation, but some general categories are gender, age, income, geography, job title, education, ethnicity, marital status, political affiliations, etc.)	
Psychographics (As above this needs to be customized for your situation, but examples are aspirations, fears, motivators, hobbies, opinions, values, life priorities, personality traits, habits, etc.)	
Proxy Products (What other products does this end user own and which does he or she value the most? Which products have the highest correlation with your target end user?)	
Watering Holes (e.g., locations, associations, online platforms—sequence them in priority and indicate intensity of each)	
Day in the Life (Describe a day in the life of the end user and what is going on in that person's head.)	
Priorities (What are your end user's priorities? Assign a weighting to each so that they add up to 100.)	_____ Weighting: _____ _____ Weighting: _____ _____ Weighting: _____ _____ Weighting: _____ _____ Weighting: _____
Feedback on Full Life Cycle Use Case	
Feedback on High-Level Product Specification	
Feedback on Quantified Value Proposition	
General thoughts/conclusions/questions the end user has	

Lessons Learned from Identifying the Next 10 Potential Customers

How did you source people to talk to in this step?

How many did you speak to?

How did you filter them to make sure they fit your End User Profile?

What was your yield rate to get to the final list (how many did you try to contact, and how many did you get useful info out of)?

Step	Hypotheses you tested through talking with the Next 10 Customers (you can test more or fewer hypotheses for each category than what are listed here)	What conclusions did you reach about the hypothesis? (Validated/Invalidated/ Still Unclear – Needs More Work)	What is your next action related to this hypothesis?
2 – Beachhead Market	1. 2.		
3 – End User Profile	1. 2.		
4 – Beachhead TAM	1. 2.		
5 – Persona	1. 2.		
6 – Full Life Cycle Use Case	1. 2. 3.		
7 – High-Level Product Spec	1. 2.		
8 – Value Prop	1. 2.		
Other Key Assumptions	1. 2. 3.		

This may seem like a simple step, but as you can see, it starts to inject a huge dose of reality into the process in a very constructive way, if you are open to it. Make sure your team is open to it as this will prove to be an invaluable course correction for your team and get you headed in the right direction with a tremendous amount of momentum and confidence if you do it properly. Remember, listening is the willingness to change your mind. Do so intelligently and based on data and real evidence as well as logic.

STEP 10

Define Your Core

WHAT IS STEP 10, DEFINE YOUR CORE?

Determine the single thing that you will do better than anyone else that will be very difficult for others to copy.

WHY DO WE DO THIS STEP, AND WHY DO WE DO IT NOW?

Having a clear definition of your Core will allow you to focus your limited resources to build and reinforce it. You do this analysis now because you now have sufficient context to understand the real driver of your value creation, so at this point you want to make sure you are situated to dominate the market you create, instead of doing all this work and investment to develop a market only to let other companies quickly reap the rewards.

By the Book: See pages 121–127 of *Disciplined Entrepreneurship* for basic knowledge on this step.
See pages 127–128 of *Disciplined Entrepreneurship* for an example of how a company addressed this step.

It is wise to build moats, but ultimately the Core is the inner sanctum that no one can get to. If they do, all can be lost.

PROCESS GUIDE

Defining, understanding, protecting, and growing your competitive advantage is essential to being a high-growth, innovation-driven company. I have worked with many companies who aspire for greatness but will fail to reach their goals without a strong Core.

The Core is that "special sauce" that would be extremely difficult for someone else to replicate if they tried to recreate your product. It is what allows your venture to deliver the benefits your customer values with greater effectiveness that any other competitor—today or in the future.

There are three fundamental elements to a strong Core:

1. **Unique:** This asset will be difficult for anyone else to replicate.

2. **Important:** This asset ties directly to your ability to produce something your target customer values very highly—specifically the Quantified Value Proposition in Step 8. You'll validate and further refine it in Step 11, Chart Your Competitive Position.

3. **Grows:** To be a strong Core, it should increase in strength over time relative to competitors.

That third element is often forgotten, and it is very important. If your advantage is that your competition does not understand what you are doing today but once they figure it out they can catch up quickly to you, that is not a Core, but instead a moat. A moat is a competitive advantage that slows down competitors but can be overcome. Moats are good, but a Core is better. A Core is an advantage that continues to put you ahead of your competitors. As such, changing it midstream can be detrimental to your company, so make sure you focus on identifying a good definition.

Defining your Core is unlike most of the other steps in the 24 Steps in that you don't have a lot of additional primary market research involved. Instead, your team looks inward and analyzes the assets and potential assets that the company has.

Use the Defining Your Core worksheet to list your assets and rank them by their relative strength. Then, identify potential moats for your business. If you have a good plan for a Core, moats can be extremely helpful to buy you time to strengthen your Core before your competitors are in a position to really put you to the test.

As you review the worksheet and start to translate your assets into a potential Core, look at *Disciplined Entrepreneurship* for several examples of good Cores—and what is not a Core, but a moat at best. Some common answers given for Core, from intellectual property to locking up suppliers, may not be a solid Core depending on your industry, and other answers, such as first-mover advantage, are almost never a Core by themselves.

It is important to keep in mind that a Core is not a benefit. It is an asset or a capability. Your customer does not really care about your internal assets or capabilities; they just want benefits (i.e., value that matters to them). For instance, lowering time to market for their own products is a benefit. If that is the desired customer benefit, the Core will be an enabling technology (a function) that creates this benefit.

Once you have selected a Core, make sure you can explain why you chose it over other options. Your Core, unlike most of the information you develop throughout the 24 Steps, cannot easily be changed without losing significant advantage in the marketplace.

Even if you are at par with your competitors today, if you feel you can gain an advantage and grow it over time compared to others, then that asset could be a great Core. That is why it is very costly to change your Core, because it is something you build over time.

In this chapter, I will provide some guidance on how to develop a game plan for a strong Core that will make your company much more valuable.

Determining your Core is a riddle that you must solve. While many other steps are dominated by primary market research and viewing the world through your customer's eyes, this step is primarily focused inward.

Moats are very valuable but do not replace the Core. I suggest you identify weak and strong moats as you think of your Core and competitive strategy.

Moats, however, can be overcome while a strong Core will be much more difficult to overcome. Your Core is your last stand to prevent others from beginning to commoditize your product or simply steal significant, if not all, market share.

To determine the Core, you will start by inventorying your asset and potential assets. You will then start to identify weak moats, strong moats, and Core candidates, ultimately choosing one. You choose only one because you do not want to diffuse your focus. One great Core is sufficient and you have limited resources. If it is strong, the value of the second is relatively unimportant. You would rather have one very strong Core than two of medium strength.

———

GENERAL EXERCISE TO UNDERSTAND CONCEPT

See the back of the book for answers to this question.

For the following companies and value propositions, identify their Core.

Exercise for Step 10: Identify the Core for Each Company

	Company	Value Proposition	Core
1	Walmart	Low cost	
2	Honda	Reliable power products	
3	eBay	Best marketplace to buy and sell	
4	Gillette	Availability with sufficient quality	
5	Oracle	Safe choice	
6	Zappos	Customer service	
7	Apple	Instant productivity	
8	Your Personal Example: _____		

WORKSHEET

Think long, hard, and creatively about what assets your team and new venture have. They can include capabilities, connections, branding opportunities, personal attributes, personal wealth, intellectual property, unique insights, key customer commitments, or something else.

Defining Your Core Worksheet

	What is your value proposition (from Step 8)?	
What assets does your team have? Prioritize from strongest to weakest.		
1.		**Strongest**
2.		
3.		
4.		
5.		
6.		
7.		
8.		
9.		
10.		**Weakest**
What are your proposed moats for your business?		
1.		**Strongest**
2.		
3.		
4.		
5.		
6.		**Weakest**
What are potential Cores for your business?		
1.		
2.		
3.		
4.		

Decision:		
1.	**What is your proposed Core from these choices?**	
2.	**Why is or will this Core be unique?**	
3.	**Why is it important to your target customer? How does it relate to your value proposition?**	
4.	**How does it grow over time relative to competitors in a way that competitors can't simply catch up once they realize it?**	
5.	**What was your second (or third) choice, and why is your first choice a better selection? Compare and contrast.**	

The decision on the Core can take a while and may seem a bit frustrating as you want to move ahead and continue to make progress. I completely understand. Isn't getting sales a great thing?

But you must understand that making sales without a Core is not sustainable if you want to be a high-growth company, because your success will only draw attention to the opportunity you have identified, and then competitors will rush in. At that point, your beautiful new venture will turn out to have been built on a foundation of sand and it will come sliding down when the first big wave hits it.

So even if you aren't sure what is the best selection for Core, pick a few candidates for the Core and realize you have to solve this riddle soon. Some of your potential Cores may end up as strong moats, but the most important thing is that you are thinking ahead and protecting yourself, and it is also highly relevant as you proceed to Step 11, Chart Your Competitive Position.

STEP 11

Chart Your Competitive Position

WHAT IS STEP 11, CHART YOUR COMPETITIVE POSITION?

Look at your product, versus your Persona's alternative options, through the lens of the Persona's top two priorities.

WHY DO WE DO THIS STEP, AND WHY DO WE DO IT NOW?

Customers don't really care about your Core. What they care about are the unique benefits to them in the areas they are most concerned about. Now that you have identified your Core, you can leverage it and your value proposition to demonstrate whether your product truly represents a breakthrough in the customer's mind.

> **By the Book:** See pages 131–135 of *Disciplined Entrepreneurship* for basic knowledge on this step. See pages 135–137 of *Disciplined Entrepreneurship* for examples of how different companies and teams have addressed this step.

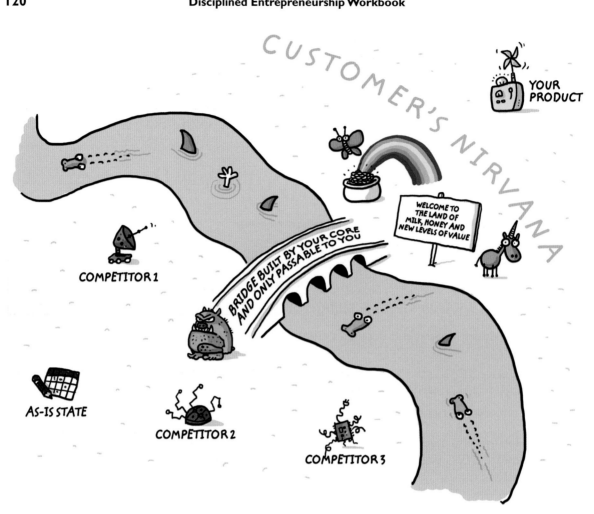

The Competitive Position shows your customer how you differentiate from the other options over the long term and shows your team why you will be a long-term success.

PROCESS GUIDE

This step spends some time thinking about your competition, but not too much. Often, entrepreneurs spend far too much time on competitors at the expense of focusing on their target customer—especially when they start doing feature-by-feature comparisons with their competitors. Remember, customers don't care about features; they care about benefits!

You must know the major competitors, especially that incredibly persistent one known as the "do nothing" option, and at some point later on you'll want to do a more robust analysis of your competition, asking holistic questions like what is the competitor's strategy, who funds them, who are their key customers, and what are the strengths and weaknesses of the leadership team.

But you're not there yet! You're still too early, and there's a lot that you need to define for your own company first. The Competitive Position is designed to quickly make sure you have fundamentally differentiated yourself from your competition and that your customer sees you are uniquely positioned to create sustainable, superior value for them. If you have properly defined a strong Core, this exercise turns out to be relatively easy.

You'll use the Competitive Positioning worksheet in conjunction with your primary market research on your Persona's top priorities. Take the Persona's top two priorities and put them on the worksheet's grid, as shown in the diagram below.

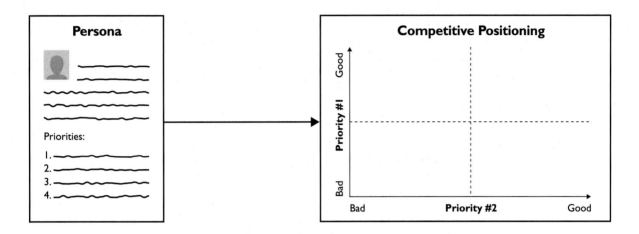

Then plot all the major alternatives the customer has, including the "do nothing" option. Options that are plotted closer to the lower-left corner are bad in all dimensions, whereas options plotted toward the upper-right corner are very attractive.

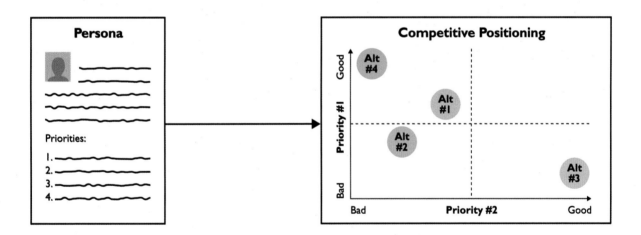

Finally, plot your position. Strengthened by your Core and your primary market research-backed work throughout the 24 Steps, you should naturally find yourself in the upper-right corner. If you are not in the upper-right corner, then you should be concerned.

If you are not in the upper right hand corner, you need to go back and revisit your Core and your market selection. Don't enter into a long battle you don't have a game plan to win.

This exercise is really quite simple, which is the benefit and the weakness of this approach as well. It gives you valuable insights to spot problems and gives you a strong general competitive plan, but there is a lot more detail you'll need once you enter the market. At that point, you will need a much more detailed competitive tactical plan to stay abreast of the competition and win.

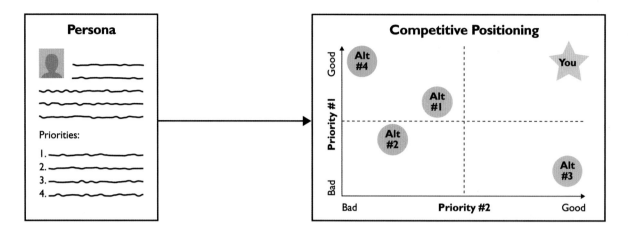

GENERAL EXERCISE TO UNDERSTAND CONCEPT

Competitive Positioning for Well-Known Companies: Choose two well-known companies and map their Competitive Positioning on the two worksheets provided below. Suggested candidates for this exercise: Uber, Apple, Airbnb, Zappos, IBM, Nordstrom, Starbucks, McDonalds, Volvo.

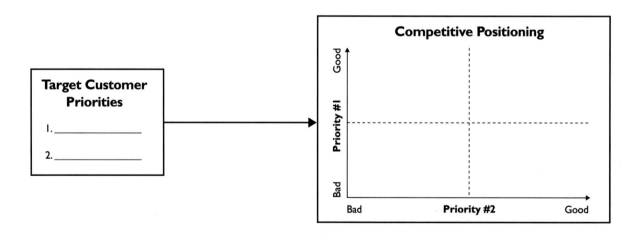

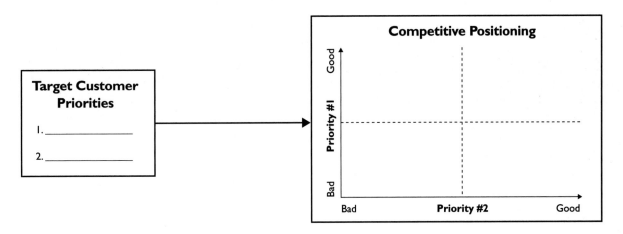

A = Do nothing option   B = _____   C = _____   D = _____   ☆ = _____

WORKSHEET

Now apply the same framework to your new venture and tie back to Step 10, Define Your Core, in the final question.

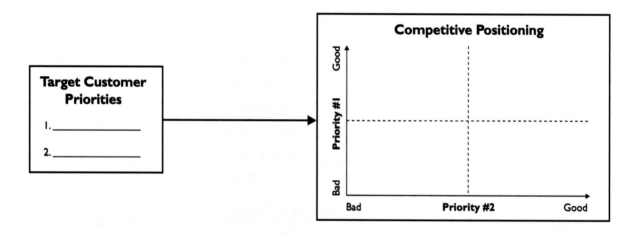

Where are you positioned relative to your competition, including the "do nothing" option? Are you in the upper-right corner? If not, why do you think that is? If other competitors are close to you on the chart, why?	What about your Core enables you to deliver so much more value that you are in the upper-right corner and your competitors are not? Explain precisely and make the linkage clear.

STEP 12

Determine the Customer's Decision-Making Unit (DMU)

WHAT IS STEP 12, DETERMINE THE CUSTOMER'S DECISION-MAKING UNIT (DMU)?

Figure out who all the people are who are involved in making the decision to purchase your product—including influencers.

WHY DO WE DO THIS STEP, AND WHY DO WE DO IT NOW?

This analysis starts the process of getting the fundamental knowledge you need to estimate your unit economics and ascertain if yours is going to be an economically viable and sufficiently attractive business.

By the Book: See pages 139–143 of *Disciplined Entrepreneurship* for basic knowledge on this step. See pages 143–147 of *Disciplined Entrepreneurship* for examples of how different companies and teams have addressed this step.

The Decision-Making Unit

There are various important roles that must be considered in every decision to acquire a new product.

PROCESS GUIDE

Having the best product or even a great one is not enough to win in business. It will generate no value and be of no consequence at all unless the end user actually gets the product and uses it. For this to happen, the customer needs to acquire the product.

"Customer" is a general term that you are now going to make much more specific. To understand the customer acquisition process, first you need to clearly identify the key people and sources of information involved. The customer is not a monolithic entity but consists of multiple roles, whether embodied in one person, or several, that constitute a Decision-Making Unit (DMU).

Once you understand who is involved in the DMU, then you can look at how to acquire a paying customer in Step 13.

The three primary roles in the DMU are:

1. **End user**: The person whose use of the product creates value for the customer.

2. **Primary economic buyer**: The person who will pay for your product and will determine whether the value the customer gets from the product is worth the cost.

3. **Champion**: The person who advocates for your product. This is the person who gets the process going and hopefully keeps it going until it is concluded.

These roles reside in actual real people and not general, unspecific organizations. Many of these roles may exist in the same person, which is common in consumer product sales. The roles may be split across three (or sometimes even more) different people in business-to-business (B2B) products.

The roles in the DMU are represented by people for the most part, but especially when it comes to influencers, they can be sources of information like *Consumer Reports* or Oprah Winfrey's television shows. In another recent development, today in some places, like the financial services, the decision is being taken out of human hands and instead made by algorithms and computers. I will consider these "robo-decision makers" not to be the norm, and as such you will not be dealing with those types of situations in this workbook.

To complete this step, use the Determine the Decision-Making Unit worksheet to copy over a summary of the most up-to-date version of the end user Persona profile, and to build Persona profiles for the economic buyer and the champion. Even if the economic buyer and the champion are the same person as the end user, prepare a customized profile for each role because the person will likely have different priorities when acting in a different role. This would also be true for any person playing more than one role in the DMU, so multiple Personas are not only allowed but recommended in such situations.

For each Persona, you should identify primary (i.e., strongest) and secondary (i.e., strong but weaker than the primary) influencers. For each Persona you should also identify who, if anyone, has veto power over the purchasing decision. Veto power can include governmental and company regulations. Remember, the purchasing department of a company is rarely an end user, an economic buyer, or a champion (although, if you are a low-cost solution, it is possible they might be a champion) and is usually only really holding veto power, despite what they might want to have you believe. Most important decisions are made by people with responsibility for the profit and loss, or at least the revenue, of a business or household, so seek them out first.

GENERAL EXERCISES TO UNDERSTAND CONCEPT

1. **Mobile phone example:** Consider a cell phone. Who is the end user of that phone? Who was the economic buyer? Who was the champion? Can you think of scenarios where this could be different? Describe those.

_____
_____
_____
_____
_____
_____

2. **Medical device example**: Assume you are selling a medical device. Who are the options to be your end user? Who are some options to be the economic buyer? The champion? Influencers of the end user? Influencers of the economic buyer? Veto power?

_____
_____
_____
_____
_____
_____

———

WORKSHEET

Determine the Decision-Making Unit (DMU)

	End User Persona (Step 5)	Economic Buyer Persona	Champion Persona
Name			
Title			
Demographic Summary			
Psychographic Summary			
Proxy Products			
Watering Holes			
Day in the Life			
Priorities (Top 4 in Order)	1. 2. 3. 4.	1. 2. 3. 4.	1. 2. 3. 4.
Key Selling Points to this Person	1. 2. 3.	1. 2. 3.	1. 2. 3.

	Primary Influencers	Secondary Influencers	Veto Power	Primary Influencers	Secondary Influencers	Veto Power	Primary Influencers	Secondary Influencers	Veto Power
People									
Organizations									
Info Sources									
Others									

How would you qualitatively summarize the DMU in three sentences or less?

_____

_____

_____

_____

_____

_____

Note that one of the limitations of this worksheet is that it is a summary. Many cells in this worksheet require a depth of knowledge that is at least a paragraph and not a few words. Another major limitation is that it is static. In reality, the roles in an acquisition process can change over time. As you map out the Process to Acquire a Paying Customer in Step 13, you may find it necessary to create additional Persona profiles to encompass the multiple stages inherent in some decision-making processes.

STEP 13

Map the Process to Acquire a Paying Customer

WHAT IS STEP 13, MAP THE PROCESS TO ACQUIRE A PAYING CUSTOMER?

Determine how the members of the Decision-Making Unit (DMU) make a decision to buy your product.

WHY DO WE DO THIS STEP, AND WHY DO WE DO IT NOW?

The Process to Acquire a Paying Customer will be a critical framework to determine the length and complexity of the sales cycle and identify critical bottlenecks in the process. Knowing the DMU has given you the prerequisite information for you to build this map. Going forward, you will rely heavily on this information to make informed decisions on designing the business model, pricing, sales channels, and ultimately your all-important Cost of Customer Acquisition (COCA).

By the Book: See pages 149–153 of *Disciplined Entrepreneurship* for basic knowledge on this step. See pages 154–156 of *Disciplined Entrepreneurship* for examples of how different companies and teams have addressed this step.

Gaining a detailed understanding of the customer's Process to Acquire a Paying Customer underlies the understanding of the drivers of the product's unit economics.

PROCESS GUIDE

In Step 12, Determining the Customer's Decision-Making Unit (DMU), you identified the "who" needed to make the purchase acquisition decision. Now you will define the "how."

You will build directly off Step 6, Full Life Cycle Use Case; however, there are two major differences. First, you will look at the same process from your perspective (the seller of your new product) as opposed to the customer's perspective, which was the case in Step 6. The two should be similar and consistent but not exactly the same. Second, this map will link directly to the players in the DMU and the customer's budgetary process. You will then use that information to develop a first draft of your Sales Funnel, which takes the information from the Full Life Cycle Use Case and turns it into an action plan for your company.

To recap, the key stages from the Full Life Cycle Use Case:

1. Determine need and catalyst to action.
2. Find out about options.
3. Analyze options.
4. Physically acquire the product.
5. Pay for the product.
6. Install.
7. Use and get value.
8. Determine value.
9. Buy more.
10. Tell others about the product.

Some of these stages may be trivial in your situation (especially for business-to-consumer [B2C] sales), but it is still worth thinking about them because even if they are small, they may well trip you up. You may also find that other stages should be included, or the stages should be listed in a different order. For instance, a customer might pay for the product before acquiring it, or after installing it, or somewhere else in the sequence. Feel free to customize the worksheet as needed, but be hesitant to remove any stages without careful thought.

You will start by filling out the Process to Acquire a Paying Customer worksheet with the descriptions of each stage from your Full Life Cycle Use Case as well as information about the acquisition process that you gain from primary market research:

- What does the customer do in this stage?
- Who is involved from the DMU?
- What are the budget limits and other considerations (governmental or company regulations, etc.)?
- How much time will this stage take? (Give a time range.)
- What is your action plan to accomplish this stage in the most efficient and effective way possible (subject to revision)?
- What are the risks?
- What is your risk mitigation strategy?
- Miscellaneous.

Next, you will convert the Process to Acquire a Paying Customer worksheet into a First Draft Sales Funnel. The Process to Acquire a Paying Customer is mapped out from the customer's perspective, but in order to define how your company will sell to the customer, you need to convert that information into a company-focused, step-by-step action plan. You will find in each step that fewer potential customers express interest, but those who are interested are far more likely to buy your product. That is why the process is expressed as a funnel that is wide at the top and narrow at the bottom.

There are many different sales funnel models, and they are all pretty similar but use different words to describe the same process. For instance, the word "lead" has many different definitions depending on whom you ask. Here are the seven elements I will use in describing the sales funnel:

Element #1: Identification—The first element is the "top of the funnel" where you generate *leads*, people who are potential customers but are not yet aware of your company. You can identify leads through membership lists for groups or associations, through watering holes, and through asking people you've spoken with during your primary market research. Once you have compared them to your End User Profile and they are a match, you call them *qualified leads*. To make things simpler going forward, however, you will simply refer to leads coming out of this element and the assumption is that they are qualified leads.

Element #2: Consideration—In this element, the lead first becomes aware that they have a problem that needs solving, and second that your product exists to solve that problem. They may develop this awareness through responding to your advertisements by contacting you, or you may initiate the first contact and they express some level of interest in your product. Once the leads have this *awareness*, they become *suspects*, and the odds of converting them to customers are much higher. Not every qualified lead will become a suspect—the fraction of leads who become suspects is called the *yield rate*. Each transition from one element to the next in the sales funnel will have its own yield rate.

Element #3: Engagement—In this element, there starts to be meaningful two-way dialogue with the suspect because the suspect shows nontrivial *interest* in your product. The suspect might express this interest through participating in a demo, submitting a request for proposal, or engaging in a substantive sales call or online interaction. Now, the suspect turns into a *prospect*.

Element #4: Purchase Intent—In this element, the prospect demonstrates a clear willingness to purchase and starts negotiating to place the order. In B2B, the prospect may discuss drafting a purchase order. In online shopping, the prospect may put your product in their basket but has not yet checked out. They are now a *highly qualified prospect*.

Element #5: Purchase—This element is the moment of truth, when the customer actually issues the purchase order and pays for your product. In online shopping, the highly qualified prospect would check out and provide their credit card information and the credit card provider confirms the transaction. The highly qualified prospect now becomes a *customer*.

Element #6: Loyalty—In this element, you focus on making sure the customer receives and installs the product, address any support inquiries that arise, and ensure that the customer is getting the expected value out of the product. Hopefully, the customer is now a *satisfied customer*.

Element #7: Advocacy—In this final element, the customer becomes a *repeat customer* and/or an *evangelist* for your product. Evangelists won't just buy more products, they'll also tell their friends and acquaintances to purchase your product, too.

Converting Full Life Cycle Use Case (Step 6) to First Draft Sales Funnel

	#1—Determine Need and Catalyst to Action	#2—Find Out about Options	#3—Analyze Options	#4—Acquire Your Product	#5—Pay	#6—Install	#7—Use and Get Value	#8—Determine Value	#9—Buy More	#10—Tell Others
Full Life Cycle Use Case Stages										
Sales Funnel Elements	**#1—Identification:** Lead Generation **Output: Leads**	**#2—Consideration:** Create Awareness to Potential Customers **Output: Suspects**	**#3—Engagement:** Develop Initial Dialogue **Output: Prospects** **# 4—Purchase Intent:** Develop Interest to Intent **Output: Qualified Prospects**	**#5—Purchase:** Close Deal and Pay **Output: Customers**		**#6—Loyalty:** Customer Support **Output: Satisfied Customers**			**#7—Advocacy:** Sell More and Positive Word of Mouth **Outputs: Repeat Customers and/or Evangelists**	

GENERAL EXERCISES TO UNDERSTAND CONCEPT

1. **Mobile phone example:** Construct a map of the Process to Acquire a Paying Customer for the mobile phone example from Step 12.

Process to Acquire a Paying Customer: Mobile Phone Example

Stage #	1	2	3	4	5	6	7	8	9	10
General Description of Stage	Determine Need and Catalyst to Action	Find Out about Options	Analyze Options	Acquire Your Product	Pay	Install	Use and Get Value	Determine Value	Buy More	Tell Others
What does the customer do in this stage? (from the Full Life Cycle Use Case)										
Who is involved from the DMU?										
Budget limits and other considerations										
How much time will this stage take? (Give a range.)										
Action plan to accomplish stage										
Risks										
Risk mitigation strategy										
Misc.										

2. **Automobile example**: Construct a map of the Process to Acquire a Paying Customer in the case of an automobile.

Process to Acquire a Paying Customer: Automobile Example

Stage #	1	2	3	4	5	6	7	8	9	10
General Description of Stage	Determine Need and Catalyst to Action	Find Out about Options	Analyze Options	Acquire Your Product	Pay	Install	Use and Get Value	Determine Value	Buy More	Tell Others
What does the customer do in this stage? (from the Full Life Cycle Use Case)										
Who is involved from the DMU?										
Budget limits and other considerations										
How much time will this stage take? (Give a range.)										
Action plan to accomplish stage										
Risks										
Risk mitigation strategy										
Misc.										

3. **Automobile vs. mobile phone:** Does the Process to Acquire a Paying Customer for an automobile take longer or shorter than the process for a mobile phone? What about for an ice cream cone? Why?

_____

_____

_____

4. **B2B example**: Now think about what the Process to Acquire a Paying Customer would look like for a multimillion-dollar machine for a corporation to help in their manufacturing. What would be the big differences between this example and the phone, automobile, and ice cream examples?

_____

_____

_____

Process to Acquire a Paying Customer

Stage #	1	2	3	4	5	6	7	8	9	10
	Determine Need and Catalyst to Action	Find Out about Options	Analyze Options	Acquire Your Product	Pay	Install	Use and Get Value	Determine Value	Buy More	Tell Others
General Description of Stage										
What does the customer do in this stage? (from the Full Life Cycle Use Case)										
Who is involved from the DMU?										
Budget limits and other con-siderations										
How much time will this stage take? (Give a range.)										
Action plan to accomplish stage										
Risks										
Risk mitigation strategy										
Misc.										

Convert to a First Draft Sales Cycle "Time to Complete" Analysis Summary

For all time estimates except for lead generation, use the numbers from your Process to Acquire a Paying Customer table above. Make a reasonable estimate for lead generation.

Sales Cycle Length Estimate

Sales Funnel Element	Full Life Cycle Use Case Stage	Estimated Time to Complete
#1—Identification: Lead Generation *Output: Leads*	n/a	
#2—Consideration: Create Awareness to Potential Customers *Output: Suspects*	*#1—Determine Need and Catalyst to Action* *and* *#2—Find Out about Options*	
#3—Engagement : Develop Initial Dialogue Output: Prospects and # 4—Purchase Intent: Develop Interest to Intent *Output: Qualified Prospects*	*#3—Analyze Options*	
#5—Purchase: Close Deal and Pay *Output: Customers*	*#4—Acquire Your Product* *and* #5—Purchase: Close Deal and Pay *Output: Customers*	
	Total time for sales cycle:	

First Draft Sales Funnel Worksheet

#1 Identification → Leads

#2 Consideration → Suspects

#3 Engagement → Prospects

#4 Purchase intent →
Qualified prospects

#5 Purchase →
Customers

#6 Loyalty →
Satisfied
customers

#7 Advocacy
→
Evangelists

Action plan for Identification: _____
_____
_____

Action plan for Consideration: _____
_____
_____

Action plan for Engagement: _____
_____
_____

Action plan for Purchase Intent: _____
_____
_____

Action plan for Purchase: _____
_____
_____

Action plan for Loyalty: _____
_____
_____

Action plan for Advocacy: _____
_____
_____

Qualitative Summary

1. How would you qualitatively summarize the Process to Acquire a Paying Customer in three sentences or less?

_____
_____
_____
_____
_____
_____
_____
_____

2. Which areas of this process are you comfortable that you have mapped out well?

_____
_____
_____
_____
_____
_____
_____
_____
_____

3. Which areas of this process are you concerned about that you will want to keep an eye on as you proceed?

_____
_____
_____
_____
_____
_____
_____
_____

BONUS TOPIC

Windows of Opportunity and Triggers

This is new material that was not covered in *Disciplined Entrepreneurship*.

WHAT ARE WINDOWS OF OPPORTUNITY AND TRIGGERS?

A Window of Opportunity is a time period in which your target customer (end user, economic buyer, and/or champion) will be particularly open to considering your offering. A Trigger is a specific action you take within that Window of Opportunity to create an urgency and/or strong incentive for the customer to act.

WHY ARE THEY IMPORTANT AND WHY NOW?

The Process to Acquire a Paying Customer is the foundation of your sales process, but you must understand that your customers are not equally predisposed to buying your product regardless of when you start the sales process. Knowing when your customer is most open to the elements of the acquisition process is an important consideration in effectively and efficiently executing your sales funnel to a successful conclusion.

Know your Windows of Opportunity and take advantage of them with well-designed Triggers—timing is crucial!

PROCESS GUIDE

One of the biggest challenges for any company, especially a startup, is initial customer adoption of their product, which is why you need to spend so much time dissecting that process and improving it. Getting the 1,001st customer after having 1,000 customers may not be easy, but I can assure you that it is almost always much easier than getting the first real customer. In this case, by a "real" customer I mean someone who is not a relative or a friend or a technological enthusiast who will buy one of everything. Instead, a real customer is someone who started with a clean slate and then, because of a customer pain/opportunity, subsequently found out about your product and chose to buy it to solve that customer pain/opportunity.

To get that first customer, you must overcome an enormous amount of inertia because it is significantly easier for the customer to not buy your product and keep doing what he or she is currently doing. The status quo is an extremely powerful force to overcome, especially before a product is widely accepted and people change their purchasing habits accordingly.

There exists a great analogy from physics. Isaac Newton's first law of motion begins by stating that bodies at rest will remain at rest unless acted upon by an external force. The potential customer is initially at rest and will stay so unless you find a way to start the process. Finding that catalyst to action is often the most important step in the Process to Acquire a Paying Customer—and often the most underrated.

NEWTON'S FIRST LAW OF MOTION

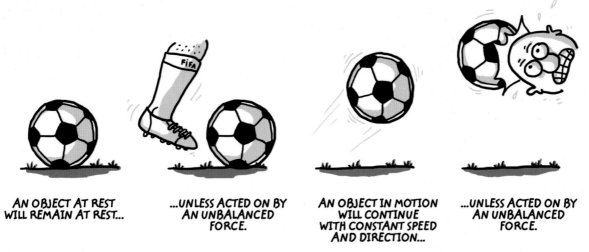

AN OBJECT AT REST WILL REMAIN AT REST...   ...UNLESS ACTED ON BY AN UNBALANCED FORCE.   AN OBJECT IN MOTION WILL CONTINUE WITH CONSTANT SPEED AND DIRECTION...   ...UNLESS ACTED ON BY AN UNBALANCED FORCE.

When you start, your customer is like an object at rest. Getting the customer to take the first step toward acquiring your product is the hardest step, so it requires special attention.

Great marketers, especially in consumer markets, have known for a long time about two concepts that will help you crystallize the catalysts to action—Windows of Opportunity and Triggers.[1]

A Window of Opportunity is a time period in which your target end user, your economic buyer, and/or your champion will be particularly open to considering purchasing your product. Examples of common Windows of Opportunity include:

- Seasonality (selling lemonade in summer and Christmas wreaths in winter)
- Crisis (e.g., blackout, security breach) or impending potential crisis (e.g., forecast for a storm, the potential Y2K computer bug)
- End of fiscal year (extremely relevant for business, but also for some consumers due to taxes)
- Budget planning cycle
- Life transitions (e.g., graduation, first job, first home, pregnancy)
- Change in leadership (e.g., company hires a new chief information officer)
- Change in regulation (e.g., enactment of the Affordable Care Act)
- Searching the Internet and finding your product (more on this later)

A Window of Opportunity only identifies a time period when you have a much better than normal chance to start the acquisition process, but it does not start the process for you. Now you need to apply that external force to get the customer moving. That is what I call a Trigger.

---

[1]Charles Duhigg discusses Windows of Opportunity and Triggers extensively (albeit with different names) in his book *The Power of Habits*, especially when he discusses the success that the superstore Target has had in using product purchase history to predict future purchases. Duhigg profiles one infamous case where Target began sending pregnancy-related advertisements to a teenage girl, prompting the girl's father to angrily complain to the store manager—only to take it back a few days later when he found out that his daughter was, in fact, pregnant, and Target had figured it out before he had.

HOW TO CREATE A TRIGGER

EXPIRING DISCOUNT　　TIME-LIMITED OFFER　　SCARCITY　　FREE STUFF　　SALES REP INTERACTION

Triggers are specific actions you take within the Window of Opportunity.

A Trigger is an action you take within the Window of Opportunity to create an urgency and/or strong incentive for the target end user, economic buyer, and/or champion to act, starting the Process to Acquire a Paying Customer. A well-designed Trigger also increases the odds that the customer will make it through your sales funnel and acquire your product. Examples of Triggers include:

1. A salesperson suddenly appearing, in person, on the phone, or in an online chat interface
2. Offering a discount that expires after a short period of time
3. Indications of scarcity of supply
4. Limited time availability to join a special community
5. Special offer of additional value to reward quick decision
6. Clear action that will help you avoid a disaster—such as a security assessment to avoid a devastating cybersecurity breach that just hit a competitor and is making headlines today

These simple concepts apply to almost every product and are extremely well known by all large corporations like Target, Google, Amazon, and Procter and Gamble. Ironically, they are even more important to entrepreneurs, who face more inertia, but these fundamental concepts are generally little known or utilized in this community. In my work, I have seen that even a well-defined Decision-Making Unit (DMU) and Process to Acquire a Paying Customer can fail if the entrepreneur does not understand their Windows of Opportunity and does not set up effective Triggers against them.

THE SALES PROCESS MAP

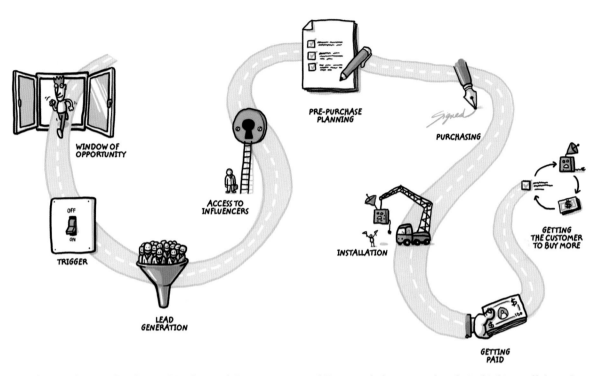

Understanding and utilizing Windows of Opportunity and Triggers help tremendously in kicking off the sales process and getting your customers to buy your product.

GENERAL EXERCISES TO UNDERSTAND CONCEPT

1. **Seasonal example:** When is the best Window of Opportunity to sell swimsuits? What Triggers do stores put in place to take advantage of that Window? Can you suggest some other creative Triggers that a store could try?

   _____

   _____

   _____

2. **Good examples to be copied**: Review the examples in the table on the next two pages and come up with other situations where the same approach could be applied.

	Company	Window of Opportunity	Trigger	Comment	Where else this approach could be tried
1	Travel website	Users come to website and look for price on a specific route, e.g. Boston to London.	Highlighted text under the price says "Only 2 seats available at this price."	Extremely effective; scarcity of supply incentivizes action now.	
2	Computer company selling high-performance and/or bulk orders of computers and/or computer peripherals (e.g., IBM)	End of fiscal year (let's assume December 31 for this example) when business departments have unspent money in their budget for the year that is just about to end—if they don't spend the money, their bosses might think they don't need the money for future years and will cut their budget accordingly.	"If you let us know in early November, we will be able to schedule our people to ensure the equipment is installed, invoiced, and paid for well before the year end so you don't have to stick around over the holidays."	Gets customer to commit to you earlier, before others who would be competing for the same funds. There may still be smaller amounts of money leftover right at year's end, so you could have another Trigger to capture that, but you have already gotten the lion's share of the available money.	
3	College student supplies company/ service	When students first arrive at school—in most places in the United States, this is late August or early September—and they form their buying habits for the academic year.	Fliers in dorms advertising giveaways and discounts that are especially attractive to new students.	Habits, once formed, are difficult to break, so smart marketers invest in the Window of Opportunity to get consumers' habits to favor them.	
4	Security company	A highly visible data breach is in all headlines.	Offer to top prospects of a special audit team to assess how exposed the prospect is, and suggest immediate plans to address the exposures.	Combines urgency of a crisis with scarcity of resources.	

#	Company	Situation	Offer	Rationale
5	Enterprise software company	New chief information officer is hired by a prospect.	Offer to review inventory of software and produce a report of where company could improve.	Regime change is a great Window of Opportunity because often everything gets rethought and new leaders want change.
6	New company that de-ices planes faster and cheaper	Right after a storm when flights got backed up and airlines were under extreme pressure because of delays; airline's customers and executives want a plan so that delays don't happen again.	Salesperson calls and explains the new offering to airlines that had the most cancellations and delays.	Having experienced significant pain, customer wants to avoid it next time, so especially open to new solutions.
7	HubSpot	A business owner visits HubSpot's website to learn about inbound marketing and HubSpot products, suggesting they are a good prospect for products that would improve the business owner's own website.	Free website grader tool that gives a numeric grade for the quality of the prospect's website with a report on what the website does well and areas to improve score—the grader also collects the prospect's contact information (e.g., e-mail address) to send the follow-up report and grade.	With the prospect's contact information and the knowledge that the prospect is interested in improving their website, HubSpot can follow up and continue to engage with the interested party.
8	Enterprise software company	One of your competitors is bought by a big company with a poor track record of customer service and integrating acquisitions into their portfolio. The new big company also has little history or expertise in the new market segment of the acquired company.	Offer a special one-time trade-in program so that users of the competitor's software can acquire your software at a steep discount. Offer free technical support for the transition for the first 20 that sign up.	Highlights your stability in a world that just got disrupted and there are new levels of risk.

WORKSHEET

Now use the following worksheet to identify Windows of Opportunity for your product and choose one to focus on. Once you have chosen the Window of Opportunity, develop a spectrum of options of Triggers for that specific Window of Opportunity and choose which one you will focus on first to test for effectiveness.

Windows of Opportunity and Triggers

	Window of Opportunity Candidates: What? When? Why?	Who is the Window of Opportunity relevant to?		
		Champion	End User	Economic Buyer
1	What: When: Why:			
2	What: When: Why:			
3	What: When: Why:			

4	What:	
	When:	
	Why:	
5	What:	
	When:	
	Why:	

Which Window of Opportunity will you target first? Why?

_____

What are potential Triggers for your chosen Window of Opportunity?

1. _____

2. _____

3. _____

4. _____

5. _____

Which of these Triggers will you test first? Why?

_____

What is a cost-effective and rapid way to test your hypothesis on your chosen Window of Opportunity and Trigger? How will you measure its effectiveness?

_____

_____

_____

_____

STEP 14

Estimate the Total Addressable Market (TAM) Size for Follow-on Markets

WHAT IS STEP 14, ESTIMATE THE TOTAL ADDRESSABLE MARKET (TAM) SIZE FOR FOLLOW-ON MARKETS?

Estimate the annual revenues from the next several markets you can start selling to after you are successful in the Beachhead Market, both by selling the same basic product to other markets and by selling the same customers additional products. This estimate represents the broader market potential.

WHY DO WE DO THIS STEP, AND WHY DO WE DO IT NOW?

This step shows the magnitude of the revenue potential your startup has, which will motivate you to focus on winning your Beachhead Market quickly and effectively so you can branch out into these other markets. It also forces you to raise your line of sight and remember you are creating a business not just for the Beachhead Market segment but for broader impact, which will affect the decisions you make about your business going forward. As the 24 Steps transition from "how does your customer acquire your product" to "how do you make money off your product," now is an opportune time to take a step back and look at the broader context for your startup.

> **By the Book:** See pages 157–160 of *Disciplined Entrepreneurship* for basic knowledge on this step. See pages 161–162 of *Disciplined Entrepreneurship* for an example of how a company addressed this step.

This step confirms and reminds you that you have bigger plans beyond the Beachhead Market.

PROCESS GUIDE

A Beachhead Market is just that, a beachhead. In World War II, when the Allies landed on the Normandy beaches, they had a very clear plan to secure their beachhead and then to move through western Europe to eventually secure Berlin and everything in between. The goal was not simply to win the beachhead territory.

The Beachhead Market gives you the all-important focus to get an initial win, build up some important credibility and capability, develop your Core, get to positive cash flow (hopefully), and start getting to critical mass for the next market. You will continue this relentless focus, but for this step now you will pick your head up and make sure you have the big picture in mind so you know that you are truly building a scalable business.

To start calculating the follow-on TAM, make a list of markets that are adjacent to your Beachhead Market. These markets should leverage your Core and fall into one of the following two categories:

- Selling your existing target customer new products, or
- Selling your base product (perhaps with modifications) to a new target customer.

You would not immediately branch out into a market where you are selling a different product to different customers compared to the beachhead. Instead, you change one variable at a time, either selling to new customers or selling new products to existing customers, so that you can rely on your strengths and knowledge from your Beachhead Market to expand. Each time you conquer a market, you can then move to an adjacent market.

Use your Market Segmentation from Step 1 as a reference if you are having trouble coming up with follow-on markets.

Once you have made this list, identify the markets that you think best leverage your Core and are in line with the passions and values of your team. Quickly estimate the number of end users and the annual revenue per user, then rank the top three markets in each category (same product and same customer) by indicating which market you would address first, second, and third.

You do not have the time to do the rigorous analysis you did in Step 4 for your beachhead, and you do not need that level of detail because by the time you get to address these markets, your priorities and the market dynamics may have changed considerably. A top-down analysis with just a quick bottom-up "sanity check" is not only acceptable but appropriate at this point.

Next, for your top follow-on market from each category (same product and same customer), make a list of markets you could pursue if you won that first follow-on market. You will quickly estimate the TAM for these markets and rank them in order of priority.

Your goal is to identify the TAM for at least five follow-on markets, so you have a better sense of your startup's potential beyond the Beachhead Market.

GENERAL EXERCISES TO UNDERSTAND CONCEPT

See the back of the book for answers to these questions.

1. **Amazon.com example:** What was Amazon.com's Beachhead Market? What have been the follow-on markets? What Core do those markets share? Have the follow-on markets proven to be more attractive than the Beachhead Market? Is that common among startups you have seen?

   _____

   _____

   _____

2. **Strategy for next follow-on market:** Where in the matrix below should you *not* go for your first follow-on market after the beachhead? Why?

   _____

   _____

   _____

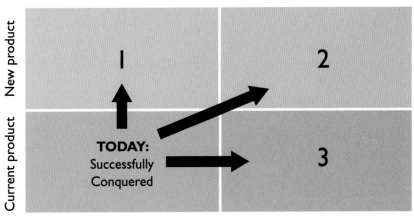

WORKSHEET

#1 (Beachhead Market): _____

Follow-on Markets:
#2: _____
#3: _____
#4: _____
#5: _____
#6: _____

Additional markets:
_____
_____
_____
_____

#1

New products for beachhead (#1) target customer → #2 → #4 → #7

New products for market #3 target customer → #5 → #8

#1 → #3 New customers for same base product → #6 → #10

New product for market #6 target customer → #9

Summary of Follow-on TAM Estimate and Priorities

Candidate	How it leverages your Core	Same product or same customer?	Pros of selling to this market	Cons of selling to this market	TAM est.	Other considerations	Rank

156

Individual Worksheet for Each Follow-on Market Segment - #2

Follow-on Market Segment Candidate Name: _____

Estimate # of users	Estimate revenue per year per user	Estimate TAM range	Compound annual growth rate (CAGR) estimate	Other considerations (profitability, time to conquer, potential market share, investment required, competition, etc.) and other comments

Individual Worksheet for Each Follow-on Market Segment - #3

Follow-on Market Segment Candidate Name: _____

Estimate # of users	Estimate revenue per year per user	Estimate TAM range	Compound annual growth rate (CAGR) estimate	Other considerations (profitability, time to conquer, potential market share, investment required, competition, etc.) and other comments

Individual Worksheet for Each Follow-on Market Segment - #4

Follow-on Market Segment Candidate Name: _____

Estimate # of users	Estimate revenue per year per user	Estimate TAM range	Compound annual growth rate (CAGR) estimate	Other considerations (profitability, time to conquer, potential market share, investment required, competition, etc.) and other comments

Individual Worksheet for Each Follow-on Market Segment - #5

Follow-on Market Segment Candidate Name: _____

Estimate # of users	Estimate revenue per year per user	Estimate TAM range	Compound annual growth rate (CAGR) estimate	Other considerations (profitability, time to conquer, potential market share, investment required, competition, etc.) and other comments

Individual Worksheet for Each Follow-on Market Segment - #6

Follow-on Market Segment Candidate Name: _____

Estimate # of users	Estimate revenue per year per user	Estimate TAM range	Compound annual growth rate (CAGR) estimate	Other considerations (profitability, time to conquer, potential market share, investment required, competition, etc.) and other comments

STEP 15

Design a Business Model

WHAT IS STEP 15, DESIGN A BUSINESS MODEL?

Consider the different ways to get paid for your product and choose the one best aligned with all of the stakeholders' interests.

WHY DO WE DO THIS STEP, AND WHY DO WE DO IT NOW?

Wise selection of a value extraction business model can dramatically reduce Cost of Customer Acquisition (COCA), increase Lifetime Value of an Acquired Customer (LTV), and provide you with a competitive advantage. It may even be the difference between your product being adopted or not. You do this now because, for the first time, you have all of the elements from the previous steps to make an informed decision.

> **By the Book:** See pages 163–171 of *Disciplined Entrepreneurship* for basic knowledge on this step. See page 172 of *Disciplined Entrepreneurship* for an example of how a company addressed this step.

Amount of time spent on
value capture innovation

Amount of time spent on
value creation innovation

Methinks you need to get things more in balance!

Entrepreneurs usually spend far too little time on analyzing and choosing a business model.

PROCESS GUIDE

I have found over and over again that when talking about "business model" with regard to startups, it is an ill-defined term, if it is defined at all. Still, it is used all the time. I want to clearly define the term for our context.

Business Model = Method to Extract Value for Your Company

The business model is your framework by which some fraction of the value you create for your customer gets paid back to your startup. It is important to understand that business model is not pricing. You will get to pricing in the next step, but you first must determine the way in which you will get paid and from whom.

The choice of a business model is a fundamental decision that entrepreneurs often make quickly with little thought. History shows that to be a mistake. A carefully crafted business model can have a huge impact on your business as well as create significant competitive advantage. More often than not, additional effort here provides a better return than spending the same effort on further enhancing your product's features. That does not mean you shouldn't have a focus on enhancing the product as well; it just means there should be a better balance. You need both.

The best way to start is reviewing some of the most common business models. See Step 15 of *Disciplined Entrepreneurship* for more information and examples on each of them. Keep in mind that creative new business models and hybrids are often created by startups to gain competitive advantage, such as the Amie Street example in *Disciplined Entrepreneurship* (page 172).

Here are some of the most common business models that companies have used:

- **One-time charge plus (potentially) ongoing maintenance agreement:** Most common.

- **Subscription or leasing model:** Now very popular, especially in the software area with software as a service (SaaS). There are numerous variants of this model.

- **Consumables:** The classic razor/razor blade model, where the initial product purchase is inexpensive (the razor), but the consumables needed to continue using the initial product (disposable razor blades) have a high profit margin. Very popular in the medical area.

- **Advertising:** Selling access to your user.

- **Transaction fee:** Earning a commission from a party for a purchase or action the user makes with respect to that party.

- **Reselling data:** Others will pay for access to information about your customers, either as a one-time download or being able to access a database on a recurring basis.

- **Usage-based:** Customer only pays when they use the product/service, but the more they use, the more they pay.

- **Cell-phone plan:** A base plan allows for a predictable monthly (or other time period) cost, and then additional ability to use the product is available at higher marginal rates.

- **Microtransactions:** Hybrid variant of per usage and one-time charge models, where users provide their credit card and then make a number of very small (often $1 or less) transactions, particularly for digital goods, that add up over time.

- **Upsell high-margin products:** A hybrid variant of consumables and one-time charge where the initial sale is for low profit or even a loss, but money is made when the customer buys optional high-margin add-on products.

- **Cost plus:** Customer pays what it costs to make the product plus some percentage of markup. Very common and not a good idea in the long term. Might make sense at the beginning but suggests that your product is a commodity, which creates a difficult environment in which to gain long-term attractive competitive advantage from. You want a business model focused on value to the customer, not cost of making the product, otherwise your business and your customer will focus on the wrong priorities.

- **Hourly rates:** A consultant or service provider model not based on costs but based on human utilization (variant of usage model). Unattractive because it rewards activity and not results.

- **Penalty fees:** An extreme variant of the cell phone plan where there is a small fee for the base service but there are substantial charges if you go over a set condition (e.g., credit card interest rates, late fees at video stores, parking meters).

- **Franchise:** You create a template for a business that others pay you for the right to implement and use your brand; you also make money by selling certified supplies and other products/services to the franchisees.

- **Shared savings:** Customer pays only after getting benefit from the product, and pays some fraction of the benefit they receive. Conceptually a good model to align customer and vendor interests, but challenging to implement, especially over the long term.

- **Operating and maintenance:** You are paid to run an operation (e.g., plant, IT services) at a fixed price, with incentives for you to make more money if you can reduce costs while maintaining service levels.

- **Licensing:** Getting paid for your intellectual property, which results in high margins but small TAM sizes. It also often results in an adversarial relationship with your customers as they tend to look at the licensing fee as a cost to be reduced each year, rather than a just payment for value gained.

- **Others:** Don't let your imagination be limited to just these models. There are always more models to be invented and hybrids to be tried. Customers are more willing now than in the past to pay based on variable pricing, as customers become more sophisticated and technology enables more options. But don't make it too complicated or it will frustrate and confuse your customers.

How should you think about what business model is right for you? There are four major areas to consider when making the decision:

1. **Value Creation**

    Revisit Step 8, Quantify the Value Proposition. How much value does your customer get? When do they get it? What is the risk that they won't get as much value as they thought?

2. **Customer**

    • Revisit Step 12, Determine the Customer's Decision-Making Unit (DMU), and Step 13, Map the Process to Acquire a Paying Customer. What is the DMU and the process? What does that analysis tell you?

    • Who gets the value? When? What is their capacity to pay?

    • Does the economic buyer favor one-time charges (called "capital budgets" in business) or smaller ongoing charges (called "operating budget" in business)?

    • What are the current standards and habits the customers have, and how entrenched are those habits?

    • Are there any showstoppers in the DMU or process that you have to be especially aware of? Examples of showstoppers may include: reimbursement or purchase authorization limits, standards, regulatory limits, onerous purchasing processes if certain choices are made, etc.

3. **Competition**

    • What business models do your competitors have?

    • How entrenched are your competitors?

    • Could you gain a competitive advantage with your target customer by using a different business model than your competitors use?

    • Could your competitors respond to that? How difficult would it be for them to do so?

4. **Internal Sales, Profitability, and Operations**

    • Will the business model decrease or increase friction in the sales process, thereby increasing your COCA? (More on this topic in Step 18, Map the Sales Process to Acquire a Customer, and Step 19, Estimate the Cost of Customer Acquisition (COCA).)

    • How do you optimize how much value you get from an individual customer over the length of time they are a customer with you? (More on this topic in Step 17, Estimate the Lifetime Value (LTV) of an Acquired Customer.)

    • If you will be dependent on distributors, will this model work for your distributors?

    • What will be the operational considerations to implement this business model? In systems? In billing? In the receivables area? Customer support? Elsewhere?

    • What kind of access to capital do you have? How will this business model affect your access?

Three final notes:

• First, business models are not easy to change once you commit to one, so think through your decision carefully before you lock into a business model.

- Second, "freemium" is not a business model; it is a customer acquisition strategy. The business model shows who will pay (the economic buyer, some third party who wants access to your end user, etc.) and how they will pay. There has to be money transferred to your company in order for something to be a business model. Freemium only impacts your COCA.

- Third, think about what "unit" of product you charge for, because the choice of units can set your startup's business model apart. For instance, consider that commercial real estate companies have traditionally charged on a basis of square feet used. Some innovative real estate organizations today are now charging on a per-employee basis or a per-desk basis. Or consider a project some of my students are working on where they make robots that cook food. What should the units be? They can choose to sell the robots, or they can use the robots to make prepackaged meals and sell to retail stores on a per-meal basis, or they could open a restaurant and sell per meal, or charge a flat fee like at a buffet. The choice of units is an important factor in your business model.

Selecting the business model is not an easy step, but it gives you a strong foundation to make good decisions throughout exploring the theme of "how do you make money off your product."

GENERAL EXERCISES TO UNDERSTAND CONCEPT

See the back of the book for answers to these questions.

1. **List to identify business model:** Identify the business model for the following:

   a. HP printer division

   _____

   b. Automotive companies (not named Tesla)

   _____

   c. Salesforce.com

   _____

   d. LinkedIn

   _____

   e. iTunes vs. Spotify

   _____

2. **Effect assets have on business model:** A startup does not have a lot of money, nor does it have access to money through banks, investment, or other means. What models does this generally favor and disfavor for the startup? Can you think of something creative you can do with a disfavored model to make it more attractive in this case?

   _____

   _____

   _____

   _____

———

WORKSHEET

Key Considerations in Choosing a Business Model

CUSTOMER

Looking at the DMU, what is important? _____

Process for acquiring a paying customer? _____

Preference for upfront (capital) or recurring (operating) expense? _____

Other considerations? _____

_____

_____

_____

_____

VALUE CREATION

How much value do they get? _____

When? _____

How risky is it? _____

Other considerations? _____

_____

_____

_____

_____

COMPETITION

Who is the competition and what business model do they use? _____

_____

How locked in are they? _____

Could I disrupt the industry? Risks? _____

Other considerations? _____

_____

_____

_____

INTERNAL

Effect on sales cycle? COCA? _____

LTV? _____

Distributors? _____

Cashflow? _____

Operations & other considerations? _____

_____

_____

_____

Identification of Different Units of Product You Can Charge For (if appropriate)

What are the different potential units you could charge for (e.g., individual product, number of users, usage, site license)?

1. _____ Pros: _____ Cons: _____

2. _____ Pros: _____ Cons: _____

3. _____ Pros: _____ Cons: _____

Summary of Business Model Candidates

#	Option	Unit	Cust. Fit	Value Creation Fit	Comp. Fit	Internal Fit	Pros	Cons	Grade
1									
2									
3									
4									
5									

Note: Do not forget to consider creative hybrid models if appropriate.

1. **Initial Decision and Rationale**

   Which business model did you choose and why?

   _____

   _____

   _____

   _____

2. **Tests to Validate**

   a. What hypotheses are you assuming to be true for the business model(s) you have chosen?

      _____

      _____

   b. What experiments will you run to test your hypotheses?

      _____

      _____

   c. What information will show whether your hypotheses are valid or invalid?

      _____

      _____

   d. How long will you give the experiments to run?

      _____

      _____

STEP 16

Set Your Pricing Framework

WHAT IS STEP 16, SET YOUR PRICING FRAMEWORK?

Determine a framework to test pricing for your new product, and make a decision on what the initial price will be.

WHY DO WE DO THIS STEP, AND WHY DO WE DO IT NOW?

Small changes in pricing can have dramatic impact on your profitability, so there is great incentive to get this right. It should also be a price that is acceptable to you and your customer so that you have a sustainable business. You are able to do this step now because you have made your initial decision on business model, and the pricing framework flows from the decisions you made in your business model.

> **By the Book:** See pages 173–179 of *Disciplined Entrepreneurship* for basic knowledge on this step. See page 179 of *Disciplined Entrepreneurship* for an example of how a company addressed this step.

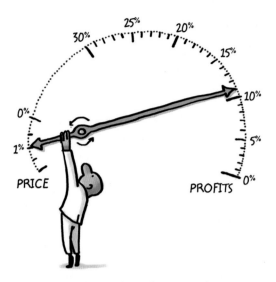

Even though it is impossible to know the right pricing for your new product just yet,
you will do some analysis now and make some decisions to get started, but also build a framework to address the
pricing decision as you move forward.

PROCESS GUIDE

It is virtually impossible to know your optimal price for your new product until you are able to offer it at scale and see how customers *actually* respond, as opposed to what they tell you they would hypothetically do. However, pricing is extremely important as even small pricing changes yield large direct effects on your profitability. As such, it is important to spend some good time on pricing now, but not too much, because it is foolhardy to think you can come up with accurate, detailed pricing at this early stage. Like with many other steps, this first pass on pricing is just a good educated guess to keep the process moving so you can continue learning; you will update and refine this step later.

In this step, you will come up with a reasonable pricing range aligned with the business model(s) you chose in Step 15, Design a Business Model. This framework will then be used to estimate the Lifetime Value (LTV) of a new average customer to your startup, and will be the starting point for later market testing (specifically, some form of A/B testing).

There are six major criteria to consider when making the decision, some of which also factored into your decision on business model:

1. **Value Creation**

   You will base your pricing on the value you create for your customer, and not your costs. While it greatly depends on the strength of your Core, think of 20 percent of the value created as a good starting point for what you can fairly capture.

2. **Customer Acquisition Analysis**

   - Revisit Step 12, Determine the Customer's Decision-Making Unit (DMU), and Step 13, Map the Process to Acquire a Paying Customer. What is the DMU and the process? What does that analysis tell you?

   - Understand what authorization limits exist for the person who pays you, and try to stay below them so you decrease friction in the sales process. If your economic buyer, who clearly understands your value proposition, can't make a purchase of $1,000 without running it by a vice president who is removed from the purchase process and will need persuading, then seriously consider pricing at $999 or lower.

3. **Nature of the Customer**

   Understand how the *elasticity of demand*, or willingness to pay, depends on the type of customer. Using Geoffrey Moore's guide from *Crossing the Chasm*, customers typically fall into one of five groups, each of whom will respond differently to different prices:

   - Technological enthusiast (this type buys based on technology coolness and as such is price inelastic and buys in low volume)

   - Early adopter (this type buys based on ego because he or she wants to be first and show off and as such is price inelastic and buys in low volume)

   - Early majority (this type buys based on compelling return on investment [ROI] and as such is willing to take risk if reward is high enough and will buy in relatively large volume and be influential)

   - Late majority (this type buys based on ROI but is willing to take less risk, will buy a good volume, and as such is influenced by success of early majority customers, which de-risked the product for the late majority; when this type finally buys, it will buy in relatively large volume)

   - Laggard (this type buys based on defensive position because to not buy is now risky because everyone else is buying, and seeks to avoid risk above all else; as such, when this type finally buys—which will be late—it will buy in relatively medium volume)

4. **Strength of Your Core**

   Your Core will be critically important in your ability to command a premium price. As it grows over time, so will your power to command higher prices and give out fewer discounts.

5. **Competition**

   Awareness of competitive options (from the eyes of the customer, not you) is an important data point to consider in this process.

6. **Maturity of Your Product**

   - Is your product new to the market, or is it a mature product that may have even been proven in other markets?

   - The former is high risk and hence harder to command a pricing premium; there is less risk in the latter, which affects not only list pricing but your ability to avoid having to discount.[1]

   - Flexibility early on, especially to get those key lighthouse customers or influential customers, is critical, and you should be willing to decrease your price in such scenarios. In such cases, customize the offering and include a confidentiality clause in the agreement with the customer with regard to the pricing so you don't set a dangerous precedent and have to provide discounts to other customers, too.

   - When you start going after follow-on markets, your success in other markets will allow you to price with fewer discounts than with your beachhead.

---

[1] Discounting is effectively decreasing the price, but it is less transparent to the market. This is in general a practice to be discouraged, but it can be a valuable tool to use in certain situations, especially early in the product's introduction to the market.

Remember it is easier to drop the price than to raise it, but that does not mean you should always start high and drop the price over time. In some cases, exactly the opposite is the better strategy, particularly with companies that have a short time window to achieve a Core of network effects.

There is also a tremendous amount of behavioral economics involved in pricing, especially for consumers. It is worth reading books and blogs on this topic. One of my favorites is *Predictably Irrational* by Dan Ariely. You should also learn more about A/B testing so that you have a fundamental skill needed to optimize pricing going forward.

After you complete your pricing analysis, you will probably be even less comfortable with the pricing decision than the business model decision. However, pricing is easier to change than business model, and you almost undoubtedly will change your pricing. Your goal for now is to make a first guess so you can analyze the unit economics for your product and see if they are viable to develop a scalable business. You'll start that analysis with the next step, Step 17, Estimate the Lifetime Value (LTV) of an Acquired Customer.

———

GENERAL EXERCISES TO UNDERSTAND CONCEPT

See the back of the book for answers to these questions.

1. **Responsibility for Setting Pricing:** While input should unquestionably come from all parties to analyze and ultimately determine prices, who should ultimately decide on pricing? Why and why not for the others?

   a. Sales

   b. Finance

   c. Product Management

   d. Engineering

   _____

   _____

   _____

2. **The Love of Nines:** Why do gas prices almost always end with as many 9's as possible?

   _____

   _____

   _____

3. **The Power of Pricing and Not Discounting:** If you increase your price by 1 percent, how much effect do you think that will have on your bottom-line profit?

   _____

   _____

   _____

————

WORKSHEET

Considerations in Setting an Initial Pricing Framework

CUSTOMER DMU/PROCESS TO ACQUIRE CUSTOMER

Looking at the DMU, what is important? _____

Process for acquiring a paying customer? _____

What spending limits are there? _____

Other considerations/Summary? _____

_____

_____

_____

NATURE OF CUSTOMER

What is the customer segment? Techie (tech) ___ Early adopter (ego) ___

Majority (ROI, some risk) _____ Late majority (ROI, low risk) _____

Laggard (avoid risk) ____ . How do you know? _____

Often it is %s & then how will you ID each type in your customer sement?

_____

Other considerations? _____

_____

_____

VALUE CREATION

How much value do they get? _____

When? _____

How risky is it? _____

Other considerations/Summary? _____

_____

_____

_____

_____

COMPETITION

Who is the competition and what are their prices? _____

_____

Which is the best comparable? _____

What does that indicate your price range should be? _____

_____

Other considerations/Summary? _____

_____

_____

STRENGTH OF CORE

How strong is your Core today compared to the competition? _____

_____

Will it get stronger over time? If so, when? _____

Do you believe you will be able to raise prices in the future? If so why? ___

_____

Other considerations/Summary? _____

_____

_____

MATURITY OF YOUR PRODUCT

Has your product & value proposition been validated in the eyes of the customer? _____

Do they see your company as high risk? _____

What kind of flexibility can you do for your first customer to decrease the real risk & perceived risk in the market? _____

Operations & other considerations? _____

_____

_____

1. **Initial Decision and Rationale**

   a. What unit of product are you using for pricing (carried forward from Step 15, Design a Business Model)?

   _____

   b. Based on your analysis, what is the price range that is most appropriate and why?

   _____

   c. In the first year, what do you believe your initial listed price will be, and what will be the effective price to the market and why? (The effective price is the actual price your customer pays after discounts.)

   _____

   d. Sanity Check: What is your expected estimated marginal cost (cost to produce a unit of product, excluding one-time setup costs)? Does your price per unit significantly exceed your estimated marginal cost in the long term?

   _____

2. **Test to Validate**

   a. In setting your pricing framework, what hypotheses are you assuming to be true?

   _____

   b. What experiments will you run to test your hypotheses?

   _____

   c. What information will show that your hypotheses are valid or invalid?

   _____

   d. How long will you give the experiments to run?

   _____

STEP 17

Estimate the Lifetime Value (LTV) of an Acquired Customer

WHAT IS STEP 17, ESTIMATE THE LIFETIME VALUE OF AN ACQUIRED CUSTOMER?

Estimate the total profit you will get from a new customer, on average, over the time period that the customer would stay with you.

WHY DO WE DO THIS STEP, AND WHY DO WE DO IT NOW?

The LTV is an important number because you will compare it against your Cost of Customer Acquisition (COCA) to see if your startup will make more money from a customer than it costs to advertise and otherwise convince a customer to buy your product. As a rule of thumb, LTV should be at least three times greater than the COCA in order for you to be profitable, though this factor varies wildly from industry to industry. Knowing what drives LTV will help you make smart decisions about your product. The LTV can now be estimated because of the work you've done in Step 15, Design a Business Model, and Step 16, Set Your Pricing Framework.

By the Book: See pages 181–190 of *Disciplined Entrepreneurship* for basic knowledge on this step. See page 190–193 of *Disciplined Entrepreneurship* for examples of how different companies and teams have addressed this step.

It may seem complicated, but COCA is just an estimate that will help you understand the critical drivers behind your company's financial success.

PROCESS GUIDE

Now that you have chosen a business model (at least an initial one) and a pricing range in the previous two steps, you can develop an estimate of approximately how much a new average customer is worth to you. You will not know this number to great precision, but it is essential to understand the general order of magnitude and what drives the profitability of a new customer. Is it the initial sale? Consumables? Retention rates? Gross margin? Volume? Repurchases? Timing of purchases?

Common inputs to estimate the LTV include:

- One-time revenue (the initial purchase price of a product)
- Recurring revenue (maintenance contracts, etc.)
- Other revenue (e.g., upselling)
- Gross margin for each revenue stream (price of your product, minus production costs—do not include sales, R&D, or administrative expenses in this number)
- Retention rate
- Life of product
- Repurchase rate
- Cost of capital for your business[1] (not for you personally, but for your business)

---

[1] Cost of capital is essentially the interest rate you will be required to pay to get more money for your new venture.

Once you know these numbers, you can build the five-year profit stream for your product. There is one last important step that you need to do. You will need to convert this revenue stream into one number with a consistent unit. That consistent unit will be "today's dollars." Today's dollars means the time at which you start your sales process and have to spend money to acquire the customers. As such you will then be comparing like for like when you compare LTV with COCA.

To do this conversion you will utilize a well know concept to people in finance called "Net Present Value" (NPV). Doing the calculation for NPV means that you discount future cash flows by the cost of capital based on how far into the future the cash flow happens. Cash today is better than cash a year from now. Cash a year from now is likewise better than cash two years from now.

What makes this especially important for you is that the cost of capital for your startup is so high. The reason for this is that your new venture is very risky and has few hard assets. Banks are very unlikely to lend money to your business, so you have to get it from other channels that will charge a premium for taking on this risk and extra work they will have to do to monitor their investment. These investors (usually equity investors as opposed to debt stakeholders) demand a return well beyond the banks or more traditional investment opportunities like public stocks or even venture capitalists (who will enter at a later stage but still expect a substantial return). The good news is that as you succeed, you will reduce the risk in your business and the cost of capital will come down, but at the beginning it is very high—50 percent is the number I suggest you use. In the worksheet in this chapter, I have helped you with a row that gives you a NPV discount factor for each year to take all of this into consideration.

Depending on your industry, you may find that a time period other than five years is more appropriate for your product. For instance, the LTV for customers purchasing a new power plant or pharmaceutical may not be comprehensive enough if you only look at the first five years. When determining whether to change this time period, consider first the length of the sales cycle, and second the amount of time it takes to develop your product. If you choose a different time period, you will still only make estimations based on five time periods—for instance, if you choose 10 years as your time period, then each interval will become two years, so that "t=1" on the worksheet becomes two years, "t=2" becomes four years, and so on.

The LTV tells you the unit profitability of how much you will make by acquiring one additional customer, minus the marginal costs—that is, the parts and labor—of making the product(s) that customer will buy. The LTV does not include marketing or sales costs, which you will estimate in Step 19, Estimate the Cost of Customer Acquisition (COCA); nor does it include research and development costs to develop the product. It also does not include the general and administrative costs (things like executive team, real estate, legal, human resources, and other overhead functions, most of which are fixed costs) required to have a company to support the overall operations.

There is great detail on how to estimate the LTV in the *Disciplined Entrepreneurship* book, so I will not repeat all that information here. I encourage you to review the material and use it as a reference when completing the worksheets below.

GENERAL EXERCISES TO UNDERSTAND CONCEPT

See the back of the book for answers to these questions.

1. **Pet Rock:** In 1975, Gary Dahl is credited with inventing the Pet Rock. It sold for $3.95 and provided a pet that required no maintenance. It became a craze, but then it died almost as

quickly and there was no lasting company. It seemed to be a failed business idea. Why do you think that is?

_____

_____

2. **Estimate the LTV and the Drivers:** Estimate what you think the LTV range is for customers of the following businesses and what drives them:

   a. Google

   _____

   _____

   b. Bicycle shop

   _____

   _____

   c. Used-car dealership

   _____

   _____

   d. A new Lamborghini sales and service dealership

   _____

   _____

━━━━━

WORKSHEET

Inputs to the Worksheet

One-Time Charge(s)

What will your one-time charges be for each customer (e.g., initial purchase price of product)? _____

What is your estimated profit margin on your one-time charges? _____

$$(\text{One-Time Charge} - \text{Marginal Production Cost})/\text{One-Time Charge} = \text{Profit Margin}$$

For example, if your one-time charge is \$100 and the cost to make that one unit of product is \$20, your profit margin is (100-20)/100 = 80%). (General estimate is fine; don't add more precision than is appropriate at this point—it can be misleading.)

What is the life of the product before a customer has to repurchase the product? _____

What percentage of customers will repurchase? _____

What will your recurring revenue streams be? _____

What is your profit margin on your recurring revenue streams? _____

What is your retention rate for your recurring revenue streams?

After first year: _____

After second year: _____

After third year: _____

After fourth year: _____
After fifth year: _____

What other revenue sources will you have? What will your profit margin be, and is there a yearly retention rate applicable to them?

_____

_____

What will your cost of capital be, and why? (If you don't know, assume 50 percent. If you do know, explain below why you think your cost of capital will be different.)

_____

_____

Calculations to Estimate the LTV

Input	t = 0 (Today)	t = 1 (1 year)	t = 2 (2 years)	t = 3 (3 years)	t = 4 (4 years)	t =5 (5 years)
A. One-time revenue amount						
B. One-time revenue profit margin (%)						
C. One-time revenue profit (row A * B)						
D. Recurring revenue amount						
E. Recurring revenue profit margin (%)						
F. Recurring revenue profit (row D * E)						
G. Other revenue amount						
H. Other revenue profit margin (%)						
I. Other revenue profit (row G * H)						
J. Sum of profit for time period						
K. Default cost of capital factor: Discount factor to NPV (@50%/year and assuming units of time = years)[1]	1.0	.67	.44	.30	.20	.13
L. NPV of each item (row J * K)						
M. Sum of all NPVs (sum of all cells in row L)	_____					

---

[1]To calculate the present value (PV) of a future value of cash (FV) where i = the interest rate and t = units of time past, the formula is $PV = FV * (1 / (1+i)^t)$

Interpretation of Estimation

1. What would you round your LTV estimation to? What range do you feel comfortable with?

_____

_____

_____

2. Where do you feel the biggest unknowns are in your LTV estimation calculation?

_____

_____

_____

3. Does the number seem reasonable?

_____

_____

_____

4. What are the key drivers of the LTV if you want to increase it?

_____

_____

_____

5. Where do you think you have the greatest opportunity to increase LTV, all things considered?

_____

_____

_____

Wow, that was probably exhausting and you feel you had to make a lot of assumptions that may turn out to not come true. They won't all come true, count on it. Still, it is better to try to plan for the future and understand where the current path will take you with reasonable assumptions.

As U.S. president and highly decorated general Dwight D. Eisenhower said, it is the knowledge gained from planning that is much more important than the plan itself. You certainly don't want to go into battle with a new product and no plan and just a belief that it will all work out, because if you had spent some time analyzing first, you would have been able to eliminate a lot of plans and paths that would be unlikely to work.

Now you will take your knowledge forward from the LTV and craft a general direction that has a path to success and glory.

STEP 18

Map the Sales Process to Acquire a Customer

WHAT IS STEP 18, MAP THE SALES PROCESS TO ACQUIRE A CUSTOMER?

Visually show how you will create and fulfill demand for your product over the short term, the medium term, and the long term.

WHY DO WE DO THIS STEP, AND WHY DO WE DO IT NOW?

The sales process is a critical input to estimating the Cost of Customer Acquisition (COCA) in Step 19. The sales process, including selecting your sales channels, will allow you to understand the unit economics of your product and then adjust accordingly to increase profitability. You can intelligently map the sales process now that you have an estimate from Step 17 of the Lifetime Value (LTV), which helps indicate which sales methods are affordable and practical for your startup.

> **By the Book:** See pages 195–201 of *Disciplined Entrepreneurship* for basic knowledge on this step. See page 201–202 of *Disciplined Entrepreneurship* for an example of how a company addressed this step.

Figuring out how to generate demand and to fulfill it with a sales channel strategy is your next key decision.

PROCESS GUIDE

Now that you have a general range for what the LTV is going to be for your product, you can now start to focus on your sales strategy. In *Disciplined Entrepreneurship* I chose not to call it a channel strategy because the decision should be more thoughtful than a typical channel strategy, but most people still recognized it as a channel strategy. I won't fight this nomenclature too much, but I think of it as a "channel strategy plus." It is a dynamic go-to-market strategy to both create demand and then fulfill demand, which are two quite different processes.

There are four main categories of sales channels to consider:

Option	Pros	Cons
1. **Field Sales:** Direct salespeople who are employees of the company. They call on prospects in person at some point in the process. They provide high-touch connection and line of communication to the potential customer. Also known as "outside sales."	• Excellent for demand generation when creating new markets; may well be the only option for demand generation • High-touch approach creates excellent feedback loop • High-touch approach also generally creates deep customer loyalty	• Very expensive (salary, bonus, expenses) • Requires an LTV of \$30K or likely higher • Hard to scale up as hiring them is hard and expensive and the success rate is unpredictable • Takes a long time to become productive • A challenge to manage

2. **Inside Sales:** Also known as "telesales" in the past, but today no longer just telephone sales reps. They use e-mail and other electronic communication to create and continue a dialogue with the customer, but do not visit the customer in person.	• Much cheaper than field sales • Maintain direct connection with prospects, potential customers, and customers • Able to get nuanced feedback from prospects because a human is in the loop • High productivity because of lack of travel • Good systems exist to further increase productivity and track progress of sales funnel and sales reps	• Lower touch, resulting in less customer engagement and less demonstration of the company's commitment to the customer • Still expensive because the salesperson is interacting one-on-one with customers • Some products just can't be sold without an in-person demo or meeting with the customer
3. **Internet Sales:** This is a general catch-all category for sales done by computers through automatically generated e-mails, big data analysis, social media, preference engines, etc. The key differentiator is that there is no human in the loop.	• Direct interaction with the customer • Ability above all others to systematically capture even more data on the customer and track their progress—as well as spot patterns and make intelligent recommendations • Lowest cost by far • Actually preferred by some prospects	• Low touch • Can't read some nuances that only humans can • Some prospects do not react well to it • Privacy considerations • Can be hard to build customer loyalty • Risk for high LTV prospects/customers that others who use the higher touch channels above will steal these valuable customers
4. **Third-Party Resellers:** These people sell your product but are not employees of your company. They include Value-Added Resellers (VARs), distributors, stores, catalogues, independent sales agents, etc.	• Instant geographic coverage • Easy to manage • Understand cultural context and have preexisting contacts in their databases • Lower cost than field sales • Don't have to hire, fire, and manage salespeople • Good for quick demand fulfillment • Potential temporary solution • Potential good solution for a mature product	• They own the customer, not you (very bad!) • Unlikely to have direct interaction with prospects, hence miss important learning about customer needs • Poor at demand generation • Expensive compared to inside sales and Internet sales • Most likely low loyalty to you and your product (just another product in their portfolio)

Within each of these four categories, there can be many different variants, as well as hybrids across the categories. For instance, someone in field sales often spends a reasonable fraction of time on the phone, but their training and expertise is in face-to-face closing the sale, and their pay reflects that.

Other than those caveats, this table will be useful to start to frame your options because it will help you determine what sales strategies are affordable based on your LTV:

Estimated LTV	What you can afford for sales channels in the long term
~$30	Only Internet sales; no human can be in the loop.
~$300	Predominantly if not all Internet sales, with maybe a very small amount of inside sales for the most important prospects.
~$3,000	Mix of Internet sales and inside sales and maybe some third-party resellers, especially if the product is mature or requires low support.
~$30K	Mix of all channels, with heavy reliance on inside sales and judicious use of field sales on big accounts. Third-party resellers can play a role in this scenario for geographic coverage and quick scale-up.
~$300K	Likely led by field sales, with support from inside sales and some third-party resellers in selected areas for geographic coverage.
~$3M	Dominated by field sales, with other channels in a supporting role.
~$30M	The field sales representatives are the all-powerful dictators; other sales channels don't even look at highly qualified prospects or customers without their approval. Customer intimacy and professionalism is crucial in this scenario.

To map your sales process, you will start by determining for the short, medium, and long term what proportion of sales will come from different channels. Use the Sales Channels for the Short, Medium, and Long Term worksheet to define the periods of time and proportions, as well as sales goals to achieve during that period, and assumptions and risks involved. You will also define what milestones you need to reach during each period so that your company is prepared to shift to the sales strategy for the next period.

Short term, medium term, and long term are defined in large part on the progress you make on your product. In the short term, you are figuring out what your product is and creating demand; in the medium term you are refining your product and starting to produce it in a repeatable fashion, fulfilling demand, and building the manufacturing and sales infrastructure you need to be successful; and in the long term, you are scaling your business. The key is that you define and understand what milestones allow you to shift your approach from the short-term sales channels to the medium term to the long term. Typically, short term will map to the first year from your LTV calculation, medium term the second year, and long term the third year and beyond, but this may differ if your product has significantly longer or shorter development cycles, such as new pharmaceutical development.

As is explained in more detail in *Disciplined Entrepreneurship*, the short term is where you will focus on demand generation and creating market awareness, and you will also still be iterating on your product and marketing, so field sales will be important despite its higher costs. As you progress through the medium term and then the long term, your sales channels should shift away from focusing on field sales, particularly for an LTV less than $1M in the medium term and less than $100K in the long term.

Next, you will take the sales funnel work you did in Step 13 and refine it into second draft sales funnels, one for each of the short-term, medium-term, and long-term time periods. Now that you know which sales channels are viable—and more important, not viable—for the long term, you have enough information to be much more specific than in your original draft from Step 13. Like everything, you will continue refining your sales funnels over time.

You'll also think through what techniques and actions you can use to maximize conversion between steps. Be creative and draw on the work you've done so far in the 24 Steps as well as ideas from other companies and industries. At the end of this chapter, I've provided an example from one of my student teams to inspire you.

A disclaimer: These worksheets are comprehensive and may be overdesigned for your situation. Or, if you have a complicated, multisided market, they may be underdesigned. Use common sense and customize this framework to fit your customer/product scenario. For instance, if you are business to consumer (B2C), some of this detail is not necessary, though I would argue it is still good for you to go through all the details so that you fully understand the big picture. Knowledge is a good thing—if you have the time.

GENERAL EXERCISES TO UNDERSTAND CONCEPT

See the back of the book for answers to some of these questions.

1. **Personal experience with a consumer product:** Identify a product in your personal life that you enjoy buying. Quickly map the experience you had in going from having initial interest in the product to purchasing it. Why do you like the sales process so much? Which sales channels does the product's maker use? Which tactics are effective?

   _____

   _____

2. **Personal experience with a business product:** Do the same exercise in #1 but now with a product from your professional life. What are the differences?

   _____

   _____

3. **Learning from negative experiences:** Now think of a product where you were particularly unhappy with the sales experience. What did you not like? What was fundamentally flawed in the sales process? How could it have been redesigned to benefit both the customer and the company selling the product?

   _____

   _____

4. **LinkedIn example:** How does LinkedIn get new customers? How do they get customers to fill in their profiles? How do they encourage customers to increase the number of connections they have on the social network? Do customers ever speak to anyone who works at LinkedIn?

   _____

   _____

5. **Private jet sales process:** Now imagine you were going to buy a private jet. (Nice!) What kind of sales process would you expect? Why?

   _____

   _____

Sales Channels for the Short, Medium, and Long Term

	Short Term—Initial Market Entry	Medium Term—Gaining Market Traction	Long Term—Steady State
How long—when does this time period start and end? (Include units—e.g., months, years.)			
What % of the sales (measured by revenue) for:			
- Field sales	____ %	____ %	____ %
- Inside sales	____ %	____ %	____ %
- Internet sales	____ %	____ %	____ %
- Third-party reseller	____ %	____ %	____ %
Key milestones for this time period, which, when achieved, indicate it is time to move to the next time period:	1. 2. 3.	1. 2. 3.	1. 2. 3.
Key assumptions:	1. 2. 3.	1. 2. 3.	1. 2. 3.
Highest risk factors:	1. 2. 3.	1. 2. 3.	1. 2. 3.
Summary for time period:			

2nd Draft Sales Funnel Inputs

		Short Term	Medium Term	Long Term
#1: Identification (Output: Leads)	How will you generate leads?			
	What are your customer's watering holes?			
	Who from the customer's DMU is involved in this part of the funnel?			
#2: Consideration (Output: Suspects)	How do you start the initial dialogue with your leads?			
	What windows of opportunity or triggers exist?			
	Who from the DMU is involved?			
#3: Engagement (Output: Prospects)	How do you determine whether your value proposition is appealing to the customer?			
	How do you determine whether your pricing is in line with the customer's budget?			
	Who from the DMU is involved?			
#4: Purchase Intent (Output: Qualified Prospects)	How do you qualify that the customer is ready to purchase, and how do you develop a proposal for the purchase?			
	How do you close the sale and handle customer questions/objections?			

(continued)

	Short Term	Medium Term	Long Term
	Who from the DMU is involved?		
#5: Purchase (Output: Customers)	How do you secure full commitment from the customer to purchase your product?		
	How does your customer pay for your product? Who pays?		
	Who from the DMU is involved?		
#6: Loyalty (Output: Satisfied Customers)	How do you ship and install the product?		
	How do you provide support to the customer so they use and get the expected value out of your product?		
	Who from the DMU is involved?		
#7: Advocacy (Output: Evangelists)	How do you encourage the customer to buy more product?		
	How do you encourage the customer to tell others about the product, and how do you measure whether customers are telling others about your product?		
	Who from the DMU is involved?		

2nd Draft Sales Funnel with Actions for Short Term

Funnel Stage	Actions
#1 Identification → Leads	Lead generation: _____ Watering holes: _____ Who: _____
#2 Consideration → Suspects	Find out about options - Initial dialogue: _____ WoO/Triggers & confirms general value proposition: _____ Who: _____
#3 Engagement → Prospects	Analyze options I - Confirms value proposition for them: _____ Confirms budget: _____ Who: _____
#4 Purchase intent → Qualified prospects	Analyze options II - Qualify & proposal _____ Verbal close & objection handling _____ Who: _____
#5 Purchase → Customers	Physically acquire product I - Secure full commitment (e.g. purchase order): _____ Pay for product: _____ Who: _____
#6 Loyalty → Satisfied customers	Physically acquire product II - Ship/install _____ Customer support - use, get value, determine value _____ Who: _____
#7 Advocacy → Evangelists	Buy more: _____ Tell others: _____ Who: _____

Describe the major differences between the short-term and medium-term sales funnels:

_____

2nd Draft Sales Funnel with Actions for Medium Term

#1 Identification → Leads

Lead generation: _____

Watering holes: _____

Who: _____

#2 Consideration → Suspects

Find out about options - Initial dialogue: _____

WoO/Triggers & confirms general value proposition: _____

Who: _____

#3 Engagement → Prospects

Analyze options I - Confirms value proposition for them: _____

Confirms budget: _____

Who: _____

#4 Purchase intent → Qualified prospects

Analyze options II - Qualify & proposal _____

Verbal close & objection handling _____

Who: _____

#5 Purchase → Customers

Physically acquire product I - Secure full commitment (e.g. purchase order): _____

Pay for product: _____ Who: _____

#6 Loyalty → Satisfied customers

Physically acquire product II - Ship/install _____

Customer support - use, get value, determine value _____

Who: _____

#7 Advocacy → Evangelists

Buy more: _____

Tell others: _____

Who: _____

Describe the major differences between the medium-term and long-term sales funnels:

_____

2nd Draft Sales Funnel with Actions for Long Term

#1 Identification → Leads

Lead generation: _____

Watering holes: _____

Who: _____

#2 Consideration → Suspects

Find out about options - Initial dialogue: _____

WoO/Triggers & confirms general value proposition: _____

Who: _____

#3 Engagement → Prospects

Analyze options I - Confirms value proposition for them: _____

Confirms budget: _____

Who: _____

#4 Purchase intent → Qualified prospects

Analyze options II - Qualify & proposal _____

Verbal close & objection handling _____

Who: _____

#5 Purchase → Customers

Physically acquire product I - Secure full commitment (e.g. purchase order): _____

Pay for product: _____ Who: _____

#6 Loyalty → Satisfied customers

Physically acquire product II - Ship/install _____

Customer support - use, get value, determine value _____

Who: _____

#7 Advocacy → Evangelists

Buy more: _____

Tell others: _____

Who: _____

Describe the major differences between the medium-term and long-term sales funnels:

_____

Techniques and Actions to Maximize Yield Rate at Each Stage

Short Term: Summary of Techniques and Actions to Maximize Yield

Stage in Funnel (starting at top)	Technique(s)	How to Maximize Conversion	Done by Whom? When?
#1—Identification (leads)			
#2—Consideration (suspects)			
#3—Engagement (prospects)			
#4—Purchase Intent (qualified prospects)			
#5—Purchase (customers)			
#6—Loyalty (satisfied customers)			
#7—Advocacy (evangelists)			

Medium Term: Summary of Techniques and Actions to Maximize Yield

Stage in Funnel (starting at top)	Technique(s)	How to Maximize Conversion	Done by Whom? When?
#1—Identification (leads)			
#2—Consideration (suspects)			
#3—Engagement (prospects)			
#4—Purchase Intent (qualified prospects)			
#5—Purchase (customers)			
#6—Loyalty (satisfied customers)			
#7—Advocacy (evangelists)			

Long Term: Summary of Techniques and Actions to Maximize Yield

Stage in Funnel (starting at top)	Technique(s)	How to Maximize Conversion	Done by Whom? When?
#1—Identification (leads)			
#2—Consideration (suspects)			
#3—Engagement (prospects)			
#4—Purchase Intent (qualified prospects)			
#5—Purchase (customers)			
#6—Loyalty (satisfied customers)			
#7—Advocacy (evangelists)			

Risk Factors

What are your three biggest risk factors in your go-to-market plan? How do you intend to mitigate those risks? What metrics will you use to monitor them and intervene as needed? (Remember, things never go exactly the way you want them to or as you plan them!)

1. **Risk factor #1 and mitigation plan:**

   _____

   _____

   Metrics to watch:

   _____

   _____

   Potential intervention strategy:

   _____

   _____

   _____

2. **Risk factor #2 and mitigation plan:**

   _____

   _____

   Metrics to watch:

   _____

   _____

   Potential intervention strategy:

   _____

   _____

   _____

3. **Risk factor #3 and mitigation plan:**

   _____

   _____

   Metrics to watch:

   _____

   _____

   Potential intervention strategy:

   _____

   _____

   _____

EXAMPLE

GearUp was a class project by Anusha Paliwal, Jillian Ardrey, and Monique Guimond—all MIT Sloan MBAs from the class of 2017. They are all avid outdoors types, and they developed a plan for a new venture that would offer an annual subscription service to provide active young traveling professionals with high-quality ski, snowboard, camping, and backpack gear delivered to them when they went on vacations. Here is how they explained how they would maximize conversion between stages of the funnel, and how they defined their milestones for moving from the short-term to medium-term to long-term sales strategies.

Sales & Marketing Efforts (1)

Technique	How Maximize Conversion?	Done by Whom, When?
Inbound marketing	Create content (blog, video) about how to travel and get outside cheaply, best destinations to add onto your work trip, destinations close to major airports, teaching outdoor skills –which target market will be searching. Buy relevant Google search terms. Conduct continuous A/B testing with content and search terms to optimize.	Marketing personnel Short, medium & long term
SEO addressing pain point	Buy Google search terms to capture potential customers searching for solutions to "how to pay less to travel with gear" or "rentals with more selection and better quality" – as our product is a solution for their pain point. Conduct continuous A/B testing to optimize.	Marketing personnel Short, medium & long term
Social media marketing	Connect inbound marketing content to Facebook & Twitter company pages and place ads on Facebook. A/B testing to optimize Facebook ads.	Marketing personnel Short, medium & long term
Articles and ads in blogs / Online magazines	Work with well-known outdoor, travel and traveling professional bloggers, as well as key magazines in these spaces, to get coverage through posts/articles. Advertise on sites of key magazines. Maximize conversion by proper targeting of sites where key user spends time.	Marketing personnel Founders (for interviews) Short, medium & long term
Field marketing	Push unique value-add of our product and engage with potential customers for advice on product iteration and optimization. Buy booths at huge outdoor events (e.g. Warren Miller premier, ski expos) and sponsor select social events (e.g. beer, music fests) in key cities and outdoor destinations. Attend relevant meetup and club events in key cities.	Founders (Short term, as interaction and feedback from customers critical at beginning) Marketing personnel (medium & long term) Don't plan to ever conduct enough field work to justify hiring full-time salesperson

Sales & Marketing Efforts (2)

Technique	How to Maximize Conversion?	Done by Whom, When?
Key travel partnerships (e.g. Airbnb, ski resorts, Expedia)	Partner with sites where potential customers go to book lodging, etc., for trips to become part of their booking process and/or advertise. Maximize conversion by partnering with the largest players where most of our potential customers book their travel. Non-hands on marketing technique which can yield strong results but will take capital, so not good for short term. Need to run pilot tests to prove ROI for this expensive marketing option.	Founders (critical relationship requiring high-touch, high level support) Medium & long term
Special pricing during windows of opportunity	Will have discounted pricing structures in place in the short term to drive growth. Price discounts will be marketed the month before each sport season starts, the holiday season, and when gear typically goes on sale at the end of each season and will require a person to book within 24 hours of receiving promo code to get discount. We will also have special pricing for our gear shop (selling discounted gear) spread via email marketing to current customers once we reveal this product feature in 2017.	Marketing personnel Short & medium term Long term, should be industry standard and not need to discount; however, re-evaluate monthly based on competition.
Ambassador Program	Current subscribers get account credits or can be entered to win trips for every friend that they get to sign up for our subscription service with their referral code. We will then contact top adopters of our referral service and provide them with marketing collateral and invite them to help us market to local meetup groups and clubs; they will get credit for everyone they provide their referral code to in these groups who subscribes to our product. This incentivization will accelerate WOM and increase conversion of those who hear about our product. Will increase % of people participating in program and referring friends through email marketing campaigns.	Marketing personnel Short, medium & long term
User Feedback Program (for optimal product selection and operations)	Critical to ensure that our Core is maintained: that we can reliably provide our customers with the gear they want and deliver it when they want it. If we don't focus on continual iteration based on customer feedback, our churn rate will rise. Will increase % of people participating through email marketing campaigns.	Marketing personnel Short, medium & long term

Evolving Sales Process

	Short Term	Medium Term	Long Term
Phase Length	*Year 1*	*Year 2*	*Year 3 and onward*
Phase Goal	*This phase will continue until word of mouth becomes significant and product selection/delivery method is optimized and proven (our core is solid). Then we will move from demand creation to demand fulfillment in the Medium Term.*	*This phase will focus on acquiring new members without direct involvement through pushing our Ambassador Program. We will continue our User Feedback Program through all phases to ensure our core stays strong. We will field interview requests and contribute to articles written about us by key media. We will roll out our gear shop (for buying discounted gear) this year and will focus on converting current subscribers to purchasers.*	*This phase will focus on acquiring new members without direct involvement through pushing our Ambassador Program and leveraging strategic partnerships. We will continue our User Feedback Program through all phases to ensure our core stays strong. We will still drive some basic marketing. We will re-evaluate our product vs. competition on a continual basis and expand into new offerings.*

This has been another intense chapter, but you are building up great knowledge of your business; so not only do you know if it is worth doing, but you also have a plan to make it great. Just as important, you are understanding the underlying drivers so you can intelligently and quickly identify and make adjustments once the business starts. It is hard work, but it will pay off. The only thing harder is trying to launch a new product and not having a good plan. That is not only more work in the end, it is much more frustrating. Hang in there, you are about to pull it all together and launch this rocket ship.

STEP 19

Estimate the Cost of Customer Acquisition (COCA)

WHAT IS STEP 19, ESTIMATE THE COST OF CUSTOMER ACQUISITION (COCA)?

Estimate the total marketing and sales expense in a given period to get new customers and divide that total expense by the number of new customers. This will be the marketing and sales expense required to acquire one additional average customer for the given time period.

WHY DO WE DO THIS STEP, AND WHY DO WE DO IT NOW?

The unit economics are a simple but effective indicator for how sustainable and attractive your business will be at any point in time and, maybe most important, as it scales. You just completed a meaningful go-to-market plan in Step 18, and that is the critical input to estimate your COCA.

By the Book: See pages 203–211 of *Disciplined Entrepreneurship* for basic knowledge on this step. See page 211–217 of *Disciplined Entrepreneurship* for examples of how different companies and teams have addressed this step.

*COCA is a tough number to estimate, so entrepreneurs often just bypass this step—
but that is a big mistake, as your business will be flying blind if you skip the COCA estimation.
Entrepreneurs also, almost without fail, underestimate COCA.*

PROCESS GUIDE

You have done an enormous amount of work in this workbook so far, and now you can tie it all together to see if the unit economics work. Very often they don't initially, but don't lose hope because now you will understand the underlying drivers of COCA and Lifetime Value (LTV), which will enable you to make adjustments to make the unit economics work. If, after the adjustments, they can't work, then don't waste your time trying to defy math and move on to another opportunity, wiser for the experience. You need to know there is some path to greatness, or at least success. Otherwise, don't go forward with the journey.

To estimate the COCA, you will take the plan from Step 18, Map the Sales Process to Acquire a Customer, and build a forecast of how many customers you expect to gain during the short-term, medium-term, and long-term time periods, as well as the total marketing and sales expenses for each time period that would result in gaining the number of customers you forecast.

To forecast the number of customers you expect during each time period, you need to do a sales forecast that you and your team really believe is not only possible but also likely. Have your forecast reviewed and tested by a sales professional. Often entrepreneurs' forecasts are incredibly naïve and wildly overoptimistic.

Your sales forecast for your first 90 days, and possibly even for your first year, should have specific names of the customers whose sales you are going to record. If the potential customers don't already know you and you know them, it is highly unlikely that they will be buying during this initial time period. Take the number of people you think will be buying and only record a percentage of that on your forecast so that it is more realistic (maybe 80 percent, but that will vary by situation).

In the longer term, your sales forecast can make more abstract estimates based on growth rate, sales productivity, and market share, but understand that the more abstract the assumptions are in the calculation of the forecast, the less credible and the more risky they are. For every story of an entrepreneur exceeding their projections, there are dozens of entrepreneurs who underachieved. Follow the maxim "underpromise and overdeliver" when it comes to your forecasts. Don't delude yourself into believing you have a great business when the facts indicate otherwise. Enthusiasm is good, but naïveté is bad. Again, get a professional salesperson to review your forecast with you so they can point out the flaws. Listen to them carefully!

To forecast your sales and marketing expenses, you will need to first estimate, based on your sales process from Step 18, what all of your sales and marketing activities will be, and how much they will cost. Marketing expenses will generally be the set of expenses that build brand awareness and generate leads, and sales expenses relate to converting those leads into paying customers.

Sales expenses may include:

- Salaries of salespeople
- The time you and other nonsalespeople spend on sales activities
- Commissions
- Bonuses
- Travel and entertainment expenses
- Benefits (health insurance, etc.) and employer taxes (social security, Medicare, etc.)

Marketing expenses may include:

- Salaries of marketing employees (and bonuses, benefits, employer taxes, etc.)
- The time you and other nonmarketing employees spend on marketing activities
- Websites
- Social media
- Advertising
- Trade shows
- Public relations
- Consultants

If some people aren't collecting a salary or their salary is below market rate, you should take the market rate for that person when calculating the expense. It is not sustainable to not pay salaries, so using anything less than market rate in your calculations will significantly understate your expenses.

If you have not done an exercise like this before, understand it will take some time to go through at the level of detail and thought required to produce a relatively accurate list of expenses. I strongly recommend you work with someone who has experience building a marketing and sales budget to help you, because otherwise you will miss a lot of expenses. Also look at the expenses that your competitors and others in similar markets incur. While you actively and aggressively seek ways to save money and be more effective by being innovative in how you approach marketing and sales—see the Dollar Shave Club example from *Disciplined Entrepreneurship*—understanding what your competitors do will ensure you are not overlooking any expenses that you will need to incur later.

I have provided a relatively blank worksheet for you to list your expected expenses, because each company will have a very different list depending on what their industry and sales channels are.

Some of your marketing and sales expenses may be related to customer retention and support, instead of new customer acquisition. Do not include those expenses in the calculation of COCA. Customer retention expenses, within reason, are generally money well spent, because your most profitable customers are almost always your existing customers—you have already spent the money to acquire them, and the costs to retain them are not nearly as high as the costs to find new customers. You don't want to lose your existing customers!

Then, take the grand sum of all the marketing and sales expenses, less customer retention and support for each time period, and divide by the number of new customers in that same time period. That will be your COCA for that time period.

In the remaining worksheets, you will look at ways you can reduce your COCA, graph your LTV against your COCA for each time period to see if your COCA is currently low enough compared to your LTV, and then look at risk factors related to your COCA calculation and how you can mitigate them.

If you stay focused on your target customer and do all the steps well, you should generate positive word of mouth in the advocacy stage of the sales funnel (see Step 18), and that will be the biggest driver to reducing your COCA in the long term.

GENERAL EXERCISES TO UNDERSTAND CONCEPT

See the back of the book for answers to these questions.

1. **Current example—LinkedIn and Groupon:** Who do you think has a lower COCA, LinkedIn or Groupon? Which direction do you think the COCA of each company is headed (up or down) and why?

   _____

   _____

2. **Dropbox example—B2C to B2B:** Dropbox is moving from strictly a business-to-consumer (B2C) business model for its products to now having a focus on business-to-business (B2B) selling into enterprises. What do you think this will do to their COCA? Do you see any challenges?

   _____

   _____

3. **Amazon.com and COCA:** How does Amazon.com keep its COCA so low?

   _____

   _____

4. **Gillette vs. Dollar Shave Club:** Why is Gillette's COCA so high and Dollar Shave Club's initial COCA so low, despite selling the same product, razors and razor blades? (See the discussion about Dollar Shave Club in *Disciplined Entrepreneurship* for background information.)

_____

_____

_____

_____

WORKSHEETS

Assumptions for COCA Estimation

What time intervals did you define for the following phases in the Step 18 worksheet "Sales Channels for the Short, Medium, and Long Term"?

Short Term _____

Medium Term _____

Long Term _____

Total Sales and Marketing Expenses List

List the expected sales and marketing expenses, and their costs. This input will be used when estimating the Cost of Customer Acquisition (COCA).

Sales Expenses	Short Term	Medium Term	Long Term

Marketing Expenses	Short Term	Medium Term	Long Term

Estimate the COCA

	Time Period (default is year but can customize)				
	Year 1	Year 2	Year 3	Year 4	Year 5
New customers forecasted					
All sales expenses for period					
All marketing expenses for period					
Total marketing and sales expenses for period					
COCA for the period					

Convert Estimation into Short, Medium, and Long Term

Understanding these numbers are not precise, estimate your COCA for the short, medium, and long term, based on the time periods you defined in the first worksheet. Make an estimate that you are comfortable with, and express the estimate as a range instead of an exact number.

    Short-term COCA range _____

    Medium-term COCA range _____

    Long-term (steady state) COCA range _____

Key Drivers of COCA and Ways to Decrease It

#	Item	Effect	Action Possible to Decrease	Risk
1				
2				
3				
4				
5				

			Example: Key Drivers of COCA and Ways to Decrease It	
#	Item	Effect	Action Possible to Decrease	Risk
1	Field Sales	High	Decrease number and increase inside sales	High in short term—need to see how market adopts product; lack of direct salespeople will definitely slow adoption
2	International Field Sales	High	Use third-party resellers	Low in short term/high in long term because we don't have direct connection with customers
3	Advertising Budget	Medium	Build up in-house social media and other capability	Medium but probably worth it in long term
4	Field and Inside Sales	Medium	Supplement and reduce numbers with stronger Internet sales investment	Medium in short term and, if works, low in long term
5	Trade shows	Medium	Eliminate and find a guerilla market approach at 10 percent of expense	Medium in that our customers expect us to be at these shows and it gives our company credibility; still something can probably be done here

Comparison of LTV and COCA over Time

Label the axes with the appropriate numbers and units, and then plot the LTV and COCA on the graph based on your calculations from this step and from Step 17, Calculate the Lifetime Value (LTV) of an Acquired Customer. Draw a line to connect the three LTV points, and another line to connect the three COCA points.

Step 19: LTV vs. COCA Over Time

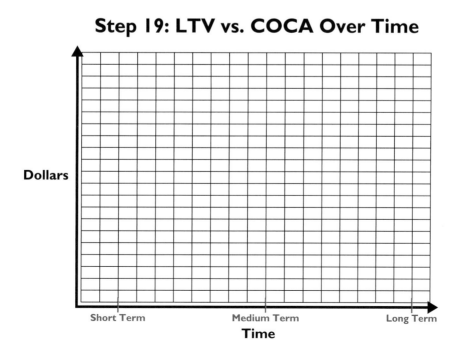

Overall Interpretation of Unit Economics—Bringing It All Together

Now that you have done all the hard work, let's pull it together and consolidate what we know and what we should do now.

1. **Basic 3X Test:** Is your LTV more than three times your COCA for your long-term time period? This is essential because COCA only deals with marketing and sales. The LTV must produce enough excess profit to also pay for research and development (R&D) as well as general and administrative (G&A) costs. The R&D costs can be significant. The 3X rule of thumb was created for software as a service companies, so the specifics of your industry may require a higher ratio in order to be successful. Does your LTV-to-COCA ratio clear the basic 3X threshold by a little, a reasonable amount, or a lot?

_____

_____

_____

_____

2. **R&D Factor:** Is your R&D expense going to be above or below that of an average software as a service company? For instance, a biotech company's R&D expenses will be much higher. If so, then your ratio needs to be higher to compensate for this. For biotech companies it can be over 100x, and for consumer goods it can be less. What is your situation, and do you feel comfortable there will be enough profit to cover R&D expenses? (G&A expenses fluctuate as well if there is a regulatory component, but they do not fluctuate as much as R&D, so we will focus on R&D as the proxy for G&A as well):

_____

_____

_____

_____

Adjustments May Be Necessary, But You Are Ready: There is a good chance that your initial unit economics don't work. Don't overreact and don't underreact. You are prepared now to go back and iterate. Go back and make adjustments like you started to list in the Key Drivers of COCA worksheet. Make adjustments until the numbers work. It is great to be passionate and that is essential, but well thought-out numbers have a stubborn way of telling the truth in business. Don't ignore them. In the end, if you can't make the unit economics work, you won't have a sustainable business no matter how hard you try. But most of the time you can fix it, now that you are equipped with this knowledge.

Once you have iterated and the plan works, like in Step 18, list the top three risk factors for the unit economics and how you plan to deal with them below:

1. **COCA risk factor #1 and mitigation plan:**

_____

_____

Metrics to watch:

_____

_____

Potential intervention strategy:

_____

_____

_____

2. **COCA risk factor #2 and mitigation plan:**

_____

_____

Metrics to watch:

_____

_____

Potential intervention strategy:

_____

_____

_____

3. **COCA risk factor #3 and mitigation plan:**

_____

_____

Metrics to watch:

_____

_____

Potential intervention strategy:

_____

_____

_____

If you are an engineer like me, you are now getting to the fun part. Now you can build the product with confidence that it can be the basis of a great company. That being said, it all makes sense, but you are not sure until it really happens. Now you move to the design and build stage in Step 20, Identify Key Assumptions.

STEP 20

Identify Key Assumptions

WHAT IS STEP 20, IDENTIFY KEY ASSUMPTIONS?

Describe the main assumptions that underpin your plan for your startup so that you can test them before the market tests them for you.

WHY DO WE DO THIS STEP, AND WHY DO WE DO IT NOW?

While you have tested many key assumptions throughout the 24 Steps, now you have all the elements of the marketing analysis plan, so now it is time to survey the full landscape and identify those key assumptions that are crucial to the overall plan before you begin to make the heavy investments in product development and the supporting infrastructure.

By the Book: See pages 219–222 of *Disciplined Entrepreneurship* for basic knowledge on this step. See page 222–223 of *Disciplined Entrepreneurship* for an example of how a company addressed this step.

*Before you push into product development, be as efficient as you can
by intelligently identifying your key assumptions.*

PROCESS GUIDE

You have reached another important milestone in your journey in that you should now be confident that you know who your customer is; that you can create substantial and meaningful value for your customer; that your target end user will acquire your product; that there is an economic buyer who will pay you as a result of the end user acquiring the product; and that the resulting unit economics will make you profitable. Congratulations!

But in the last paragraph you said "you are confident" a lot. You have self-assurance, but you don't truly know what is going to happen when you start trying to sell your product. It is now time to step back and think holistically about the biggest risks you face and how to mitigate them before you move forward to a stage where the costs and resources you expend will increase dramatically. As they say, "In concept, concept and reality are the same, but in reality, concept and reality can be very different." You need to test your conceptual comprehensive plan one last time as much as possible before the real battle begins.

All along you have been testing your assumptions with primary market research, so what is the difference now? Until now, you have not had the full picture. Now that you have completed 19 steps worth of product/market fit planning, you can identify those assumptions that stand out overall as the most critical for your success.

There is also the challenge with people that they will say one thing, even with the best intent, and then do something completely different when the decision day actually comes. This is especially true with willingness to pay, but it can also be true in other areas. So even assumptions that seemed accurate until now need to be more thoroughly tested when linked together.

Start by reviewing the work you have done in each step of the 24 Steps thus far and build a list of key assumptions you have made at each step. Prioritize the list and identify the 5–10 assumptions that are the most crucial to the success of your product. Use the provided worksheet to list these assumptions, the related step(s) from the 24 Steps, the risk level of the step (low, medium, high, critical), and briefly describe what will happen to your company if your assumption turns out to be incorrect.

In the next step, you will test these assumptions, but for now, don't worry about how you will test them, or you will be biased toward easily tested assumptions. Your goal for now is to identify the most important assumptions, regardless of ability to test them.

Here is an example of a prioritized list of top assumptions, which comes from one of my student teams:

Beehive needs to test several high-risk assumptions that could force the team to change the whole business model

#	Assumption	Related steps	Risk level	Potential Impact
1	The U.S. market is attractive to our customer base	8. Value proposition	Critical	If wrong we are not solving the right problem
2	We are able to streamline the process of opening an account in the United States	10. Core	Critical	If not possible there is no Beehive, or Beehive needs to be a investment platform for Indian markets
3	Newbees are willing to invest time and money in their financial literacy	8. Value proposition 10. Core 15. Business model 16. Pricing framework 17. LTV	Critical	If not we need to create value through giving access to U.S. market and forget about MasterBees and copy trading
4	Newbees will trust our MasterBees	5. Persona 8. Value proposition	High	If not, we must define a different value proposition (i.e., thematic mutual funds)
5	MasterBees will find interesting Beehive to gain some money	15. Business model	Medium	If not we won't evolve to a marketplace, but not a high impact in the short term because MasterBees will be paid
6	Beehive is able to give access to U.S. stock markets without becoming a license broker	10. Core 15. Business model 19. COCA	Medium	If wrong, Beehive will need to incur higher costs, and we need to rethink financials and business model
7	Newbees are willing to invest at least $5,000 in our product	5. Persona 17. LTV 19. COCA	Medium	If wrong, Beehive needs to reduce COCA and become even more a low-cost model

———

GENERAL EXERCISES TO UNDERSTAND CONCEPT

See the back of the book for answers to the first question.

1. **Segway example:** What assumptions did Segway make that in hindsight they should have identified and tested before building and launching their product?

   _____

   _____

   _____

   _____

   _____

   _____

   _____

   _____

   _____

   _____

2. **Personal example:** Identify a product you know that did not do well in the market. In hindsight, what two or three things did the manufacturer assume but should have known not to assume?

   _____

   _____

   _____

   _____

   _____

   _____

   _____

   _____

   _____

   _____

WORKSHEET

Identify Key Overall Assumptions

#	Assumption (in prioritized order)	Related step(s) from the 24 Steps	Risk level	Potential impact if assumption is wrong
1				
2				
3				
4				
5				
6				
7				

In many ways this is a "catch your breath and digest what you have produced" step. It does not not involve a lot of new work, but it is important to set yourself up for the next step as well, which is to test these assumptions. It is nice to have a step that is a bit easier, isn't it? You are getting close to the end now—hang in there!

STEP 21

Test Key Assumptions

WHAT IS STEP 21, TEST KEY ASSUMPTIONS?

Use a series of small and inexpensive experiments to test each of the individual assumptions you identified in the previous step. Be creative!

WHY DO WE DO THIS STEP, AND WHY DO WE DO IT NOW?

This scientific approach will allow you to understand which assumptions are valid, which ones are not, and which ones you can't know for sure yet. As a result, you'll have time to make adjustments to your planning while the cost and time to do so is much less than it will be in the very near future when you launch the product development process.

By the Book: See pages 225–228 of *Disciplined Entrepreneurship* for basic knowledge on this step. See page 228–234 of *Disciplined Entrepreneurship* for examples of how different companies and teams have addressed this step.

Testing your individual assumptions may not always give you the answer you wanted, but it can be fun and rewarding—and much better to find your problems before your customer does!

PROCESS GUIDE

This step ties directly back to Step 20, Identify Key Assumptions. Now that you have identified the most critical individual assumptions, you will design experiments that test these assumptions. Your goal in each experiment is to test a specific variable, keeping all other factors as controlled as possible, so that the result of your experiment gives you insight into the validity of your assumption.

Designing good experiments requires that you be systematic and think creatively. There is an entire field of research, behavioral economics, that explains why people make the decisions they make and how to design proper and efficient experiments that will illuminate this behavior, so I won't go into detail within the confines of this workbook. Instead, I suggest that you read some of the literature in this field. One book I find immensely useful in describing the value of well-designed experiments as well as the emerging field of behavioral economics and some of its basic principles is *Think Like a Freak* by Steven Levitt and Stephen Dubner, who are well-known for their bestselling book *Freakonomics*.

It should be fun to design the experiments that test your assumptions, and you don't need a team of PhD economists, especially if you're only testing one assumption in each experiment. If an experiment is more complex, such as one that tests multiple assumptions at the same time, it gets much more difficult and less fun. Hence, try to decouple assumptions and design your experiments carefully.

On the first worksheet provided, describe some detail about the experiments you plan to run, including which assumption(s) will be tested, what resources you need for the experiment, and most important, what outcomes will validate your assumption(s). If you don't define your outcomes before the experiment, you will inevitably skew the experiment in favor of your assumptions, making the outcomes worthless as indicators of the strength of your new product's plans.

After you conduct each experiment, use the second worksheet to make notes about each experiment, including the outcomes, whether your assumption(s) were validated, and what your next steps are based on those outcomes—whether that means revising work you did earlier in the 24 Steps, conducting additional experiments with revised variables, or taking other appropriate actions. Sometimes the result of a successful experiment is more experiments. You have to be patient.

See the bottom of this page for how student team Beehive approached some of the assumptions that I first showed you in the last step.

Notice how simple the tests can be. Some may be as simple as calling your vendors to validate your list of how much it costs for each part that goes into your product (the cost of goods sold), as that cost is often a key assumption. Or, if getting a certain highly influential customer in your chosen market segment is a crucial validation point, you'll want to more energetically measure their commitment level. The expectations and commitment thresholds are still low because you should not be communicating to customers that you have a product being sold—you're still in inquiry mode for a bit longer, which is a much better environment for experiments. Enjoy it while it lasts because it will be ending soon!

Make sure to also review the examples provided in *Disciplined Entrepreneurship* for this step, as some of my students have come up with very creative ways to test assumptions quickly and inexpensively.

Finally, remember that a valid assumption is still only an assumption, because only with paying customers do you truly know that your startup has a sustainable market. I will guide you through how to start determining whether customers will actually buy your product in Step 23, Show That "The Dogs Will Eat the Dog Food," and in general, an experiment that invalidates an assumption will often tell you more than an experiment that validates an assumption. Nevertheless, the more you test in advance, the more problems you can identify while fixing problems is still relatively inexpensive.

To test the assumptions, we have designed 3 experiments, 2 of them currently running

#	Empirical test	Related assumptions	Status	Resources
1	A/B testing over a landing website with signup option to preview a new investment platform that allow users to access the U.S. market (Google AdWords and Facebook ads)	1,3,4 (the campaign point at 3 different landing pages with slightly different information)	Running	Low. Done through a WordPress and spent $200 in ads
2	Opening a broker account in the United States on our behalf (international students) and on behalf of a customer in India	2,6	Opened negotiations with brokers	Medium: we need to sign up a collaboration agreement with a broker in the United States. We need cash to invest
3	Run a simulation with a paid MasterBee and at least 20 prospective clients. We will simulate how a MasterBee would give advice to clients. It could be done by using something as simple as Twitter accounts.	3,4,5	In design	Medium: Cash to pay the MasterBee, development of an MVP (it could be as simple as a Twitter account)

———

GENERAL EXERCISE TO UNDERSTAND CONCEPT

Examples from Step 20, revisited: What tests could Segway have run to test some of the key assumptions? How about for the product you identified that did not do well in the market?

_____

_____

_____

_____

WORKSHEET

Test Key Overall Assumptions

#	Empirical test (in order from most important to least important, based on the risk levels of the related assumption[s])	Related assumption(s)	Resources required for test	What outcome(s) would validate your assumption(s)?
1				
2				
3				
4				
5				
6				
7				

Results from Testing Key Assumptions

#	What did you learn from the test?	Did the test validate your assumption? (Yes, No, or Not Knowable At This Point)	What will you do as a result of this test (e.g., revisions to work done in previous steps, additional testing of assumptions)?
1			
2			
3			
4			
5			
6			
7			

After having completed this step and the previous step, you have de-risked your product at the level of individual assumptions as much as you reasonably can. This accomplishment does not mean that, when all the assumptions are put into one product, the fully assembled solution is assured of market success. In addition, some assumptions will never be able to be fully tested until there is a product and it is put into production. That testing comes in the next two steps.

STEP 22

Define the Minimum Viable Business Product (MVBP)

WHAT IS STEP 22, DEFINE THE MINIMUM VIABLE BUSINESS PRODUCT (MVBP)?

Determine what is the minimum product you can use to test whether your end user gets value from your product and whether the economic buyer is willing to pay.

WHY DO WE DO THIS STEP, AND WHY DO WE DO IT NOW?

Once you ship a product, the stakes become much higher, but the quality of feedback becomes much, much better, too—in particular, feedback about whether customers are willing to pay you for your product. But to reduce the stakes, complexity, and investment, you don't want to build out the entire product now. Keep the number of variables as low as possible by first developing a minimum product that starts an iterative feedback loop with your customers. All of the work from the previous steps builds up to this moment.

> **By the Book:** See pages 235–237 of *Disciplined Entrepreneurship* for basic knowledge on this step. See page 238–244 of *Disciplined Entrepreneurship* for examples of how different companies and teams have addressed this step.

It's time! You have done all your homework, so now you have to give your customer a product, but keep it simple to start.

PROCESS GUIDE

To create an MVBP, your goal is to do the least amount of work possible to achieve three key objectives:

1. The customer gets value out of your product—that is, you validate your work from Step 8, Quantify the Value Proposition.

2. The economic buyer pays for the product—you're probably not maximizing short-term profit yet, but you're showing a willingness of the economic buyer to pay something greater than zero.

3. You start a meaningful feedback loop with your customer so you understand what about your product works, and what is missing or needs to be refined—as well as what priority to give the work you still need to do.

While the MVBP is minimal, the customer should see it as a product at this point (hence why "business product" is in the name) and not as simply a prototype for feedback. The prototypes could come into play in Steps 21 and 22, Identify and Test Key Assumptions, but unless the customer is paying for the prototypes, they do not meet the criteria to be a product. At the same time, you're not trying to deliver a full-fledged version of your product; the MVBP is the smallest set of functionality and investment needed to get you started. Once you are successfully moving forward with regard to the three criteria above, you can then incrementally add more and more functionality.

One key tactic that startups have used to successfully demonstrate MVBPs is "concierging" elements of their solution. "Concierge" is a fancy word to say that rather than build out an efficient or comprehensive solution that requires a huge, time-consuming up-front investment, you instead deliver a labor-intensive solution that can't scale when you get larger, but requires no or minimal up-front investment. Or you outsource a noncustomer-facing part of your solution to a company that has the infrastructure in place to do so, even if you lose money by outsourcing. You could call it "fake it until you make it."

One of the greatest examples is how Amazon.com got started. Jeff Bezos and his team started by selling books, but they didn't have an inventory of books or even an agreement to resell them. That did not stop them from setting up a simple website collecting book orders. When someone bought a book, they ran out to a nearby bookstore and bought the book, almost always at a higher price than what they had advertised, and then ran to the post office to ship it. They lost money on each book.

So why did they do it if they lost money? Because it validated that the market was worth making investments in inventory and back-end logistics. The money they lost in the concierge stage was invaluable market data and education in what value customers got from their service, and what features they needed to build for their customers.

The level of detail needed for an MVBP will vary depending on your industry. I have heard software entrepreneurs say that if you are not embarrassed when you ship your first product, you shipped too late. That ethos might work well for some software, but it doesn't translate well to every situation. If you are making a product for brain surgery, for instance, your MVBP's core minimal reliability better be rock solid! It can and should have a narrow scope in terms of features and functions, but it can't fail. Much is written about software entrepreneurship and then extrapolated to other industries, so use common sense when applying startup advice to the particular demands of your industry.

To get started on defining your MVBP, first review the work you did in Step 7, High-Level Product Specification. Visually describe your MVBP on the first worksheet provided. Then, on the second worksheet, define how your MVBP meets the three key objectives for an MVBP. Finally, consider any opportunities to concierge elements of your MVBP so that you can minimize development time and focus on testing what your customers think of your product.

GENERAL EXERCISE TO UNDERSTAND CONCEPT

Concierging an MVBP: Do an Internet search to find an example of a company that concierged elements of their MVBP. (Make sure you find an example where the product fulfills all three criteria of an MVBP—customer gets value, economic buyer pays for it, you engage customer in a feedback loop.) What is their value proposition? What elements of the MVBP did they concierge? How did they plan to automate those functions in a later release? How effective was their strategy? What would you have done differently?

_____

_____

_____

_____

_____

_____

———

WORKSHEET

Update Your High-Level Product Specification

Updating Step 7, High-Level Product Specification, what features and functions do you really need for the MVBP? Will these features and functions achieve the three objectives of an MVBP? Visually describe your MVBP.

How Your Proposed MVBP Meets the Three Objectives of an MVBP

Objectives	How, specifically, does your MVBP meet this objective?
1. **Value:** Provides value to end user consistent with Step 8	
2. **Pay:** Prove that the economic buyer will pay something for the product placement	
3. **Feedback:** Creates meaningful feedback loop with customer (end user, economic buyer, and champion)	

Minimizing Investment and/or Speeding Time to Market—Concierge Opportunities

Is there anything in your MVBP that can be concierged to reduce the initial investment required to achieve the above three objectives and/or decrease time to get to market with an MVBP? Time may be even more important than money.

_____

_____

_____

_____

_____

_____

_____

_____

STEP 23

Show That "The Dogs Will Eat the Dog Food"

WHAT IS STEP 23, SHOW THAT "THE DOGS WILL EAT THE DOG FOOD"?

Offer your Minimum Viable Business Product (MVBP) to your target customer and obtain quantitative metrics regarding the adoption rate of the product, the value the customer is getting from the product, and that someone is paying for the product.

WHY DO WE DO THIS STEP, AND WHY DO WE DO IT NOW?

Numbers don't lie. Entrepreneurs have an ability to create great passion for a vision, but now is the time for reality, to show concrete evidence that your product, and specific features of it, are succeeding. Qualitative information and conceptual logic are not sufficient. You do this step now because you finally have the MVBP and you need to validate it before moving forward.

By the Book: See pages 245–248 of *Disciplined Entrepreneurship* for basic knowledge on this step. See page 248–252 of *Disciplined Entrepreneurship* for examples of how different companies and teams have addressed this step.

The customer is the final arbiter of success, so now you will build a scoreboard to show whether the customer accepts the MVBP.

PROCESS GUIDE

Entrepreneurial ventures usually fall into one of two varieties. The most common state is that they are blindly optimistic that everything is going great and getting even better. The other state is one of paranoia where the team is overly pessimistic about the launch of their first product. In either case, the entrepreneurs suffer from some of the same biases I spoke about in the primary market research chapter, and as such they don't collect sufficient appropriate quantitative postlaunch data to override the confirmation bias that kicks in to validate their original point of view. As a result, they overreact or underreact to how the market responds.

Don't fall into this trap. Be vigilant as a team to maintain the level of objectivity, specificity, and rigor you learned in your primary market research work and that you have kept throughout the 24 Steps. If you do, you will much better understand whether the level of adoption is in line with what you should be seeing.

Just like you did in Steps 20 and 21, where you first identified your key assumptions and then tested them, in this step you will test the integrated MVBP you defined in Step 22. The ultimate test now is whether the end user is using the product and getting value, the economic buyer is willing to pay, and the champion is pleased enough with the results to keep championing your product and company.

There are many different ways to quantitatively measure your adoption rate.[1] In this workbook, I recommend that for consistency, you use the framework from Step 18, Map the Sales Process to Acquire a Customer, as your initial foundational framework because it covers the full sales cycle from customer awareness all the way to repeat customers and word of mouth. The worksheet for this step presents the seven stages in the sales funnel and asks you to provide the conversion rates for each stage in the funnel, compare it to the industry average, and define other metrics useful to your startup.

Your instinctual qualitative observations can help guide you on how your product and go-to-market plan are working, but you need to combine them with quantitative data or you will be in the blindly optimistic or pessimistic world I described in the beginning of this step. Lord Kelvin expressed it memorably in saying: "When you can measure what you are speaking about and express it in numbers, you know something about it. When you cannot, your knowledge is of a meager and unsatisfactory kind."[2]

So what numbers should you look at?

1. **Initial interest**: Once your target customers are exposed to your value proposition, what percentage of them actively seek to learn more? On a website, you can measure the click-through rate from a page that details the benefits of the product to a subsequent page.

2. **Conversion rates**: Once the target customer is in the sales funnel, the yield rates going from section to section of the funnel are extremely important numbers to understand, both the absolute numbers but also the trends.

3. **Purchase and pay**: The ultimate conversion. Whether the customer pays for your product is one very important indication of whether the customer is getting value. How long it takes the customer to pay, and what percentage of customers end up not paying after making an initial commitment (the "default rate"), are also interesting numbers to watch.

4. **Retention rates**: It is always telling to monitor retention rates, often referred to in the negative modality of "churn rate," especially in subscription businesses. One way to measure retention rates is through support or maintenance contracts for postpurchase support. If the customer buys the product but doesn't sign up for a maintenance contract at the end of the warranty period, in some industries that is a bad sign and you should take note immediately.

5. **Customer advocacy**: There is a huge difference between a satisfied customer and a very happy, evangelizing one. The latter is at least one order of magnitude if not more valuable to you. The simplest and most commonly used way to measure customer advocacy is the Net Promoter Score (NPS), developed by Bain & Company, Satmetrix Systems, and Fred Reichheld. You gather the necessary data by asking customers a single question: On a scale of 1 to 10, with 10 being the highest, how likely is it that they would recommend your product to a friend or colleague? By tallying the percentage of responses that are nines and 10s ("promoters") and subtracting the percentage of responses that are sixes and below ("detractors"), you get your score, which can be as low as -100 (all detractors) and as high as 100 (all promoters).

---

[1] Dave McClure describes a good approach and specifically addresses the front end (i.e., the initial sale) of this with his "Startup Metrics for Pirates" presentation, but he does not talk about the back end (i.e., after Step 6 in your sales funnel) as much, which is critical as well. See http://www.slideshare.net/dmc500hats/startup-metrics-for-pirates-long-version.

[2] He also said, "In science, there is only physics; all the rest is stamp collecting," so while very quotable, he was certainly no diplomat.

6. **Cost of Customer Acquisition (COCA) and Lifetime Value (LTV)**: Estimate these numbers again now that you have some sales. They are much easier to estimate the second time around! They are valuable, albeit imperfect, indicators of your success. If there are surprises in these numbers, then quickly dive into them and understand why.

7. **Gross margin**: Your gross margin, the difference between what it costs to make one unit of product and what you sell that unit of product at, should go up over time, indicating that you are getting strong word of mouth for your product. If it goes down, then you are possibly providing too many discounts on your product, so the number of customers may be going up because the price is artificially low. The gross margin trend is an imperfect indicator on its own (much like the other indicators here), but make sure you monitor it.

Don't feel constrained by this list. There are plenty of other metrics that will be equally or more valuable for your situation.

While it is hard to capture all of these metrics, especially at the beginning, they will be highly useful to you, especially within the framework of the sales process from Step 18.

Before you release your product, make sure you clearly define what metrics you will be observing, how you will observe them, and what constitutes success against those metrics. In the worksheet for this step, I suggest coming up with percentages for conversion between each step of the sales funnel, as well as monitoring gross margin, LTV, and COCA. You'll also want to roughly define the time period(s) over which you'll make your initial observations, since you'll need to give customers some time to hear about and evaluate your product, but not too much time or you might expend too many resources on a product nobody wants. If you release your product without carefully defining what constitutes success, it is all too easy to pretend that whatever results you get are indicators that you have a good product. Don't fall into that trap!

GENERAL EXERCISE TO UNDERSTAND CONCEPT

Viral video and then what? A new product comes to market via a highly entertaining video that goes "viral," meaning millions of people view it over a short time period. However, very few people go to the product's website (less than 0.1 percent), and very few of those people convert to paying customers for the product, which is a subscription business (0.2 percent conversion rate of those who visited the website). How would you assess the situation? What has this company done well? What has it not done well? What should its next steps be?

_____

_____

_____

_____

_____

_____

WORKSHEET

What time period(s) will you measure metrics for (give duration and units—e.g., two weeks, two months,)? _____

Are Your Customers "Eating the Dog Food"?

Stage in funnel (starting at top)	Est. industry conversion average (%)	Your conversion goal (%)	Actual conversion rate (% and trend)	Next steps if your actual conversion rate is lower than your goal
#1—Identification (leads)				
#2—Consideration (suspects)				
#3—Engagement (prospects)				
#4—Purchase intent (qualified prospects)				
#5—Purchase (customers)				
#6—Loyalty (satisfied customers)				
#7—Advocacy (evangelists)				

Gross Margin, LTV, COCA

	Expected for short term	Actual for short term	Next steps if actual is lower than expected
Gross margin			
LTV			
COCA			

Define and Test Other Metrics

List custom metrics here:	Expected for short term	Actual for short term	Next steps if actual is lower than expected
Net Promoter Score (NPS)			

Reflections

What surprised you about what customers actually did versus what you expected them to do?

_____

_____

_____

_____

What didn't surprise you?

_____

_____

_____

_____

Summarize your action plan now that you have tested adoption of your MVBP. Do you need to revise your work from previous steps?

_____

_____

_____

_____

Congratulations on making it this far! You have broken through, and now you have to grow your beachhead and start to scale up your product and company.

STEP 24

Develop a Product Plan

WHAT IS STEP 24, DEVELOP A PRODUCT PLAN?

Describe how you will improve your product over the next several versions so that you can fully capture your Beachhead Market and then start to address follow-on markets.

WHY DO WE DO THIS STEP, AND WHY DO WE DO IT NOW?

Putting together a broader plan for your product allows your team to have a solid foundation stepping out from the 24 Steps into a more dedicated incremental product development cycle. You will continually refine the work you have done in this workbook, even though there are no more formal steps to be followed in this methodology beyond Step 24. At this point, if all of the steps have been completed, you have successfully launched your product.

By the Book: See pages 253–255 of *Disciplined Entrepreneurship* for basic knowledge on this step. See page 255–259 of *Disciplined Entrepreneurship* for an example of how a company addressed this step.

Step 24 points in the direction for your next trip, which is likely another lap through the
24 Steps for the next release of your product.

PROCESS GUIDE

Step 24 is the beginning of an ongoing and evolving plan to scale and grow your product and business from its initial success. You must think longer term beyond the Minimum Viable Business Product (MVBP) and the Beachhead Market. Each time you expand to a new market, you will need to iterate on the basic concepts behind the 24 Steps in detail if you want that market to be successful. In fact, for each new market, you will cycle through the 24 Steps again for that market to generate the detailed plan for the product for that market. Don't worry, however, because each subsequent time you execute the process, it is easier and most likely faster. For now, you will just lay out a high-level game plan.

Start by planning out features and functions for the next two versions of your product for the Beachhead Market. For purposes of this chapter, make both versions functional releases, but keep in mind that you will likely need to intersperse with releases that focus on improving the quality of existing features. At one of my hardware startups, SensAble, we defined that releases should alternate between a functional release and a quality assurance release. At Google, they use the phrase "ship and iterate" to emphasize the importance of releasing something, even if the software has bugs in it, and commit to both making improvements to the quality of the existing product and to adding new features. Make sure quality is continually addressed in the product, even if it means removing features as appropriate. Otherwise, feature releases (which are frankly more exciting) just keep coming and quality slips away.

The features and functions should be linked to specific benefits that will make your product even more invaluable to the target customer in your Beachhead Market. One of these releases may be a good opportunity to replace concierged parts of your MVBP with a more scalable solution, even if it means temporarily taking your product off the market in order to do so.

You'll also want to understand how each additional version leverages your Core. As you expand your product's capabilities, you do not want to forget the work you have done in Step 10, Define Your Core, and Step 11, Chart Your Competitive Position, because those are the key elements that will sustain your company and provide you a lasting competitive advantage. If you ignore your Core and do not strengthen it over time, you will have developed a wonderful product specification, no longer just a high-level spec like in Step 7, but a full blueprint backed by strong primary market research, only to see another company swoop in and reap most of the profit and rewards because you have no lasting competitive advantage relative to them.

Also, consider what resources are needed to develop and implement each new feature or functionality. Then, assign a priority to each feature or functionality based on how important it is to your customer, its relationship to your Core, and whether you have the available resources to pursue it at this step.

It is impossible to know exactly which of these features you will end up implementing, but you should continue to make and test assumptions related to your customer and product because careful planning will significantly increase the odds of your success. You have to be open to changing your plan as new data comes in, but if you have no plan, you will waste a lot of time trying things out without understanding the metrics for success. Great entrepreneurs mix planning and flexibility so that they can both rapidly and productively iterate. Balance is the key.

While you are planning features and functionality, also consider what other activities you will need to do in parallel with releasing new versions of your product. Perhaps there will be regulations you need to keep in mind as you expand, or you will need to invest time in providing specific services that support the end users' use of the product.

Next, consider the various follow-on markets you initially sketched out in Step 14, Estimate the Total Addressable Market (TAM) Size for Follow-on Markets. At this point, you have a lot more information than you did when you made your first pass on this question, so take another look at your candidate follow-on markets, and determine which will be the top markets for you to pursue next. Keep in mind that from your Beachhead Market, you either sell the same or similar product to a different target customer, or you sell additional products to the same target customer, and each time you conquer a new adjacent market, you can only change one of those two variables. Changing both variables will put you well outside your expertise and require you to do a level of primary market research akin to starting the 24 Steps completely over, which you do not have the time or resources to do.

Finally, you'll want to visually represent your Product Plan so it is clear to everyone on your team how your product will grow over time as it better serves the Beachhead Market and begins to serve adjacent markets. I've provided a general worksheet in this chapter, but feel free to modify as needed and do not feel constrained by the specifics. In *Disciplined Entrepreneurship* you'll see other examples of displaying a visual Product Plan that still use a graph with two axes but display the information differently. What is key is that you have a plan and that you can communicate its essence concisely, without overloading it with details.

GENERAL EXERCISES TO UNDERSTAND CONCEPT

See the back of the book for sample answers to these questions.

1. **Creating a market but not owning it:** Can you think of an example of a product where one company went in and showed the world an exciting new market, but then the company was unable to capture the benefits of its vision and execution? What do you think they could have done differently?

   _____

   _____

   _____

   _____

   _____

   _____

   _____

   _____

2. **Success story of disciplined product scaling:** Now let's look at the other end of the spectrum. Think of a wildly successful product from a startup or a bigger company. What was the product's Beachhead Market? How did they scale the product and move into adjacent markets? What can you learn?

   _____

   _____

   _____

   _____

   _____

   _____

   _____

   _____

Product Plan – Version 2 for the Beachhead Market

This plan is not a commitment, but a best-guess plan subject to change as you learn more from Version 1.

#	Feature/function	Benefit	How does it leverage your Core?	Priority	Est. resources needed to develop
1					
2					
3					
4					
5					
6					

Product Plan – Version 3 for the Beachhead Market

This plan is even less of a commitment as it is further out in the future.

#	Feature/ Function	Benefit	For whom? End user, economic buyer, champion	How does it leverage your Core?	Priority	Est. resources needed to develop
1						
2						
3						
4						
5						
6						

Other Activities beyond Functionality for the Beachhead Market

What other activities do you anticipate doing related to the product to help it scale after version 1.0 for the Beachhead Market (e.g., go-to-market activities, regulatory matters, additional complementary services to support the product, additional sales channels—anything not related to product functionality listed above)?

1. _____

2. _____

3. _____

Moving beyond the Beachhead Market—Analysis and Prioritization of Follow-on Market Candidates

For the worksheet on the next page, refer to your work from Step 14, Calculate the TAM Size for Follow-on Markets, but build upon it with the knowledge you have gained since that first draft.

Analysis and Prioritization of Follow-on Market Candidates

#	Name	Which market does it follow from?	Pros	Cons	Does it leverage your Core? (Y/N)	Priority	Key factors needed to succeed	Resources required	Risk	Reward
1										
2										
3										
4										
5										

Product Plan Overview

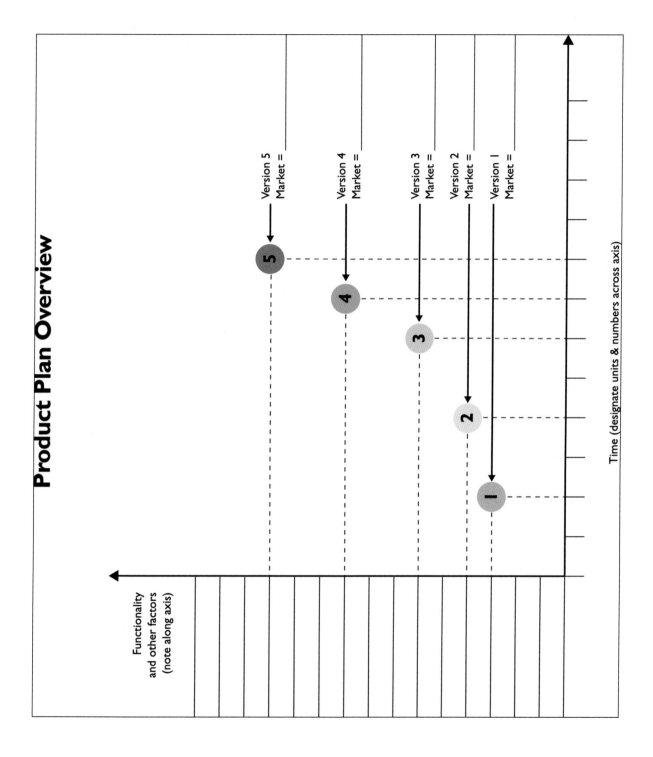

Functionality and other factors (note along axis)

Version 5
Market =

Version 4
Market =

Version 3
Market =

Version 2
Market =

Version 1
Market =

Time (designate units & numbers across axis)

Wow! The good news is that you have made it through the 24 Steps. Congratulations! That is quite an accomplishment, and you are so much better off for it. Now the bad news: It never ends. You are constantly updating what you have done. Life never stands still, nor does business. You must constantly use this framework to refresh your business so that another startup does not come along and take your market share. But more good news to end the chapter: It is much easier the second time around, and it will continue to get easier with more repetitions.

BEYOND THE 24 STEPS

WHAT IS MISSING IN THE 24 STEPS?

I always talk about the need for focus and to be clear about what you are "deselecting" when you choose what to focus on. Similarly, in order for the 24 Steps to excel at guiding you through new product development, there were so many things relevant to startups in general that I had to leave out. In *Disciplined Entrepreneurship*, I ended with a reminder about the many areas essential to a startup that the 24 Steps do not cover, such as building a company culture, selecting a founding team, growing and building the team (human resources processes), selling and sales execution, servicing the customer and building customer service processes, raising money to scale the business, entrepreneurial leadership and scaling the business, building and utilizing good company governance, and much more.

In this workbook, I want to elaborate a bit more on three key areas of focus so that you have guidance to keep your entrepreneurship education going and refreshed.

Team and Culture

As mentioned earlier, your team will be your most important factor in determining success. That does not mean you shouldn't put enormous focus on your customer and product plan (you should) as that is the best way I have found to determine whether you have a strong and aligned team. Always be aware that you must have a *great* team; "good enough" never is if you want a great company.

The customer and product plan is essential, but conditions will change and you must have a team that will adjust. As you think of different versions of your product, it is also important to think of different versions of your team, each time getting stronger. This may involve upgrading skills, adding people to the team, moving people off the team, redesigning the organization to work better, or changing responsibilities and reporting structures. You must do what is best for all the stakeholders, which includes not only the employees but also the customers and, later, investors. If someone on the team is not a good fit, you are doing no one (including that employee) a favor by failing to acknowledge the lack of fit. It does not mean the employee did not play a vital role at some point, or is a bad person, but rather they are not in a job that allows them to shine. You need to have a very coherent and skilled team to succeed in the tough world of entrepreneurship. Keep upgrading your team and have a mindset and general plan to do so, but always consider values in this decision process.

I wrote a piece on this topic for TechCrunch called "Culture Eats Strategy for Breakfast,"[1] which talks about the incredible power of a strong corporate culture and the danger of ignoring this difficult

---

[1] See https://techcrunch.com/2014/04/12/culture-eats-strategy-for-breakfast/.

topic. It also gives you some examples and references as to how to develop your own unique but appropriate culture.

With regard to a more prescriptive approach to the HR challenge of building and continually upgrading your team, I would recommend the definitive book on the topic by Noam Wasserman called *Founder's Dilemmas* and his website www.noamwasserman.com, which has assessment tools and lots of other useful materials.

Financials

In this book, you did product unit economics and you were encouraged to make a first draft marketing and sales budget, but that alone is insufficient to fully understand the viability of a business and to track progress. This analysis only briefly mentioned the investments you will need to make in research and development as well as general and administration expenses; much more needs to be done.

Sometimes people say you should not worry about the financials because all financials are going to be wrong. Yes, they will be wrong, but without a simple, dynamic model to gauge the rough magnitude of the financials, you will be flying blind in a turbulent area when you don't need to. At the outset of *Disciplined Entrepreneurship*, I state that the single necessary and sufficient condition for a business is a paying customer. That is not an accident. Money needs to come into your organization for it to be a business, and for it to be a sustainable business, you have to have more money come in than go out. Cash is the oxygen for your business; without it, you die.

So even if you know you can't get the numbers in your financial projections precisely right, it is so important that you build a general financial model to guide you in this critical area. Don't let this impossible-to-solve problem drag you down; instead, do enough to understand the underlying dynamics so that yours can be an economically sustainable business. You don't need an MBA, but you do need to be financially literate.

There are many books and financial specialists who can guide you through how to make a simple model. There is no one-size-fits-all model here that magically solves the problem, as each startup has its unique story with different cost dynamics. It is not that hard, but you have to be organized and be comfortable with numbers—or someone on your team needs to be. If you and your team are not, I warn you that business requires this skill, so you should consider putting someone on your team (at least part-time) who has an interest in and can ultimately do the financial analysis to guide you before you jump into the entrepreneurship world.

Other Functions

You will need to set up functional groups/teams for other things that need to be done to support the product getting to your customer in the most efficient and effective manner. This includes but is not limited to human resources (as per "Team and Culture" above), finance (as per the previous paragraph), customer service, marketing communications, public relations, competitive analysis, engineering, research, legal, regulatory, manufacturing, fundraising (different than financial and often overemphasized for startups—most often the best thing you can do to raise money is to have a great business), and other general services.

Setting up these functional teams within an organization is nontrivial and nonobvious. I personally got invaluable training at IBM in my early years on how to do this and the importance of organizational design. It is not something people are just born with and, in fact, it is often counterintuitive.

I suggest you seek out experienced people in designing scalable organizations and listen carefully. Sometimes success in the product area makes you believe you can easily solve this problem; that is not true. First, it requires a different skill set. Second, it is very hard to get right the first time. It is complicated because it involves humans and their motivations, so get assistance as you do this.

Conclusion

Each one of these items, as well as each part of the 24 Steps, has a rich amount of experience and research behind it. Use this book as the beginning of your entrepreneurship education, not the end. The more you know about entrepreneurship, the more you will not only control your own destiny going forward, but you will thrive in the increasingly changing and unpredictable future. Hopefully this book has given you the insight, the confidence, and the hunger to want to become a better and better entrepreneur. The entrepreneurial journey never ends, and neither should your entrepreneurial education journey.

WORKSHEET

What other activities are you going to do to continue to build your entrepreneurial skills and network?

1. _____

2. _____

3. _____

4. _____

EXERCISE ANSWERS

STEP 2

1. The beaches of Normandy, France were an ideal beachhead for the Allies because they were not an obvious choice to start the invasion, so they were less fortified by the German army. Once the beachhead of Normandy was secured, follow-on "markets" included other areas of France, followed by countries like Belgium and Luxembourg, and finally Germany.

2. Socially active college undergraduates at Harvard University.

3. Pinterest is an interesting case. They stumbled upon an "accidental beachhead" after some time of trying to find their way in any market. Before they knew it, a large proportion of their user base were women who used Pinterest's boards to plan their weddings. While Pinterest would not necessarily describe this group as their first target market, this market provided the initial lift and development of the fundamental product that would allow Pinterest to conquer additional markets.

4. Finance departments with complex calculations that required sensitivity analysis. In particular, the first spreadsheet program for the IBM PC, VisiCalc, was the "killer app" that solidified this beachhead.

5. The Apple Macintosh is another case of an accidental beachhead. It took over a year after the computer's release in 1984—where it appeared that the Macintosh never got real market traction and it seemed headed for the same fate as its predecessor, the infamous Apple Lisa—before desktop publishing (Aldus PageMaker to be precise) became available for it. Once PageMaker caught on in 1985 and it became the killer app for the new machine, the Macintosh not only dominated the desktop publishing market quickly but became the highly preferred computer of the creative professional.

6. Cell phones first appealed to wealthy people who frequently needed to be reachable while traveling, such as real estate agents and doctors who already were using pagers and were used to such mobile technology, according to cell phone inventor Martin Cooper. See Tas Anjarwalla, "Inventor of cell phone: We knew someday everybody would have one," 7/9/2010, CNN, http://www.cnn.com/2010/TECH/mobile/07/09/cooper.cell.phone.inventor/. Personally, I vividly remember a Beachhead Market for cell phones for traveling salespeople in cars, which made perfect sense to me. This likewise was a "killer app" that had a very compelling value proposition.

STEP 5

1. Studies show that the second advertisement is much, much more successful. Soviet leader Joseph Stalin is reputed to have said, "A million people die and it is a statistic; one person dies and it is a tragedy." To learn more about the power of narrative, see *Made to Stick* by Chip and Dan Heath.

2. Having led a few startups and having worked with hundreds more, I can assure you the answer is "B." You'll never figure out the absolute best strategy, even if you have all the time in the world, unless you roll up your sleeves and start trying things out. Instead, you need to focus on building a strong and committed team so you can keep moving and figure things out as you go along.

3. These spokespeople are not Personas, but rather aspirational figures who inspire and attract the real target customers. The company wants you to think they are the Persona because they want you to think that you are like these celebrities, and that you can be like these celebrities if you buy the product. The spokespeople serve in the role of heroes to the target customer, and are therefore able to influence the target customer dramatically. As you will see in Step 12, Determine the Customer's Decision-Making Unit, influencers play a strong role in any decision-making process.

STEP 6

1. B—specifically, *the right people* don't know about the app, so they never try it and they don't know what they're missing. It's the classic paradox, "If a tree falls in the woods and no one hears it, does it make a sound?"

STEP 7

2. "a" is a benefit, "b" is a feature, "c" is a function.

STEP 9

- Team 1: The team seems to have good sales skills, but they should not be selling yet because they do not have a homogeneous Beachhead Market based on these Next 10 Customers, as evidenced by how many of the customers don't match the demographics, psychographics, use case, or value proposition of the Persona. Yes, the customers have said they will buy the product, but without a well-defined target customer, the company will find it hard to gain traction due to poor word of mouth. This team needs to redo their Next 10 Customers map, and if they can't find 10 customers similar to the Persona, they need to reevaluate their whole plan, starting with the TAM.

- Team 2: The team has great focus and a homogenous set of customers. It is good to see that the customers are not family or friends (or friends of friends), meaning the customers will be less biased toward liking the product out of politeness and will provide more honest feedback. The team now needs to go talk to the rest of these customers and ascertain their willingness to purchase the product. Maybe they can use one of Team 1's salespeople to do so!

STEP 10

Each company's Core:

1. Walmart: Vendor management and logistics; worldwide sourcing and a strong purchasing organization that extracts the lowest possible prices from vendors. All of this is supported by a culture celebrating ruthless minimization of expenses.

2. Honda: Motor technology and manufacturing.

3. eBay: Network effects.

4. Gillette: Domination of distribution channels.

5. Oracle: Sales organization—existing long-term relationships, well-defined and refined sales processes, IT systems, training, compensation systems, culture.

6. Zappos: Complete top-down commitment to customer service excellence above all else, embedded into HR, operational processes, systems, measurements, culture, etc.

7. Apple: Tightly integrated products based on industrial design, hardware development, software development, and manufacturing, creating a frictionless user interface

STEP 14

1. Amazon.com's Beachhead Market was selling books. They have had a wide range of follow-on markets over time—toys and games, electronics, video games, clothing, household supplies, and many others—and many of these have proven to be more lucrative than bookselling, particularly as many used books have become available for as low as a penny plus shipping through Amazon's affiliate sellers. Amazon.com has also interestingly expanded into Amazon Web Services (making its back-end systems available to others for a price) and now they are creating their own products (e.g., Echo) and content (e.g., movies and TV shows). All of this is a long way from books, but you can see the logical progression over time.

2. Do not go to market #2. If you have to develop a new product for a new target customer, you might as well throw away your primary market research from the 24 Steps and start over, and you simply don't have the time or resources as a startup to do that.

STEP 15

1. Business models:

a. HP printers use a "razor/razor blades" model where the initial product (the printer) is cheap, and the required consumables (ink cartridges) are relatively expensive compared to the printer's purchase price.

b. Automotive companies primarily use a one-time charge (buying a car—using yearly model updates to encourage customers to sell their existing car and purchase a replacement), with additional revenue from out-of-warranty parts and services. New recurring revenue streams that these companies are trying include subscriptions to services like OnStar, updates to GPS systems, onboard Wi-Fi, and others. Look for these sorts of recurring revenue streams to increase in number. Tesla breaks the automotive mold by not updating their models every year, and I anticipate they will look more like a hardware company that charges a one-time cost for the hardware plus a recurring maintenance fee to update the software regularly, which will be a high-margin revenue stream.

c. Salesforce disrupted the software industry with a subscription/leasing model and some elements of a per usage cell phone-type plan, so that users did not need to make large up-front investments (buying server hardware and software).

d. LinkedIn has multiple streams of revenue—advertising, premium subscriptions, and reselling data to recruiters and companies looking to make new hires. Reselling of data has turned out to be the most lucrative, but the revenue streams are independent of each other so LinkedIn can keep pursuing all the revenue streams without fear that one revenue stream will interfere with the success of another.

e. iTunes started with a one-time charge model for buying individual songs. Spotify is a subscription service where a recurring monthly fee provides access to their whole catalog. When digital music first came out, customers preferred one-time charges because that was more consistent with their buying habits (CDs, tapes, vinyl records were all one-time charges). Over time, customer purchasing habits have evolved and now a subscription model has become more preferred, especially with younger buyers.

2. Lack of access to money favors one-time charges that allow for large up-front payments so the startup can fund its growth more effectively. Most other business models, such as subscription and consumables, are harder for a startup to implement, because you have to spend a lot up front with the promise of future revenue. Startups have found ways to work around these obstacles, such as encouraging prepayment of a full year subscription at a discount, like how a magazine subscription works.

STEP 16

1. Answer is C—Product management should set pricing because they have the full picture and are incentivized by both short-term and long-term success of the product. Sales is focused on short-term results; finance's role is not to try and understand market dynamics; engineering has to focus on getting the technical side working. Everyone has valuable input—sales can tell you about customer reactions, finance can assess the financial viability of the pricing, and engineering can tell you the costs and what technology is feasible to build—but only product managers or similar roles (such as the CEO at a small-enough company) has the full picture. On that note, don't give sales too much leeway in promising discounts, because sales has the incentive to "make the sale" even if it means steep discounts; too steep a discount is dangerous in the long term. Let the CEO handle strategies for discounts.

2. Behavioral economists find that consumers react favorably to products with prices that end in nines. One theory is that consumers focus on the first part of the number, so gas for

1.999/gallon seems like buying at \$1/gallon, which would be much cheaper than gas at \$2/gallon, whereas the jump from \$2/gallon to \$2.01/gallon is seen as less significant. Another theory, which MIT Sloan Professor Duncan Simester and Northwestern/Kellogg Professor Eric Anderson discuss in the *Harvard Business Review*, is that seeing a product ending in nine can make a consumer think that the price is discounted. See "Mind Your Pricing Cues," *Harvard Business Review*, September 2003, https://hbr.org/2003/09/mind-your-pricing-cues.

3. In the book *The 1% Windfall*, Dr. Rafi Mohammed shows that a 1 percentage-point increase in price increases profits by an average of 11 percent. All of your fixed costs are already set, so increasing the price further is all profit. By contrast, adding more customers also results in revenue, but offset somewhat by customer acquisition and support costs. Pricing your product at what the market can bear is important precisely because underpricing means you are leaving money on the table.

STEP 17

1. The Lifetime Value (LTV) for the Pet Rock could go no higher than \$3.95 since there were no recurring revenue streams (as the Pet Rock required no maintenance) and little customer repurchase (once you have one rock, you're pretty much set, and there was no thought about getting customers to purchase additional types of products). The actual LTV was probably \$2 since the manufacturer sold to retail stores at wholesale prices. Be wary of "one and done" products and fads, especially when the LTV is this low.

2. Order of magnitude estimates for each:

   a. Google: Tens of dollars

   b. Bicycle shop: Hundreds of dollars (initial sale of bike + accessories, service)

   c. Used car dealership: Thousands of dollars (one-time sale; little opportunity for repeat business since they are usually not in the servicing business)

   d. New Lamborghini sales and service dealership: Hundreds of thousands of dollars (initial purchase is \$200K–400K plus high-margin services and upselling)

STEP 18

4. LinkedIn almost never uses humans in the sales process to end users. Preference engines, algorithms leveraging big data, and automated e-mail follow-up with new customers take care of sales for almost all cases. Only recruiters with high LTVs are able to speak to an actual salesperson.

5. Purchasing a private jet is a classic high-touch sales process. Field sales will be heavily involved in the process because there is a large LTV, potentially with support from other channels. The representative will customize the sales process and product to your specific needs. They know that anyone who buys a jet has a lot of money, so there is a lot of opportunity for follow-on sales.

STEP 19

1. LinkedIn has a strong Core—networking effects—and value proposition, allowing its Cost of Customer Acquisition (COCA) to decrease among both users and recruiters who find the site more and more useful over time. Groupon does not have a strong Core or value proposition, since their consumers are loyal not to the website, but to the deep discounts they provide, allowing other "daily deals" websites to copy Groupon and gain market share, and the loyalty to deals means that businesses who advertise with Groupon do not get the expected volume of customers who become repeat customers, as these customers are driven by price and not other considerations. As a result, Groupon's COCA has gone up over time as they have to actively persuade more users, especially on the business side, to use their product, whereas LinkedIn has been able to reduce their COCA by relying almost entirely on automated Internet sales to keep getting new users.

2. As of the writing of this book, Dropbox was moving to business-to-business (B2B) due to a more attractive LTV, compared to the consumer market's expectation that the product is a freemium offering. Their COCA will also go up dramatically, since the Internet sales technique used for consumer sales will not be enough to gain, as customers, enterprises used to a more high-touch sales and support process. Dropbox will need inside sales, and probably some field sales, significantly increasing COCA. The sales process for selling to a business is much different than the process for selling to a consumer, and very few companies have succeeded in having two parallel sales processes. Microsoft is one exception, with success due to vastly superior resources and a core monopoly on its consumer side. I hope Dropbox succeeds, but it is a daunting challenge!

3. Amazon.com is on the leading edge of Internet sales—preference engines, algorithms on big data sets, targeted and personalized e-mail offers, etc., and no humans in the sales loop.

4. Gillette spends heavily on advertising and setting up a dominant distribution strategy through retail stores, to the point where their Core is their distribution channels. They achieved massive economies of scale and used their market power to raise prices and increase functionality, resulting in rapid product obsolescence that kept customers buying and kept the LTV growing. Dollar Shave Club realized that the retail store strategy was not the only way in a world where customers were increasingly comfortable with buying household products online, and through innovations like leveraging social media (see Step 19 in *Disciplined Entrepreneurship* for how their initial video, "Our Blades are F***ing Great," disrupted the market), they were able to enter the market at a low COCA and build their brand. No wonder Unilever bought them for $1 billion within five years! In fact, it's possible that Dollar Shave Club missed an even bigger opportunity by not developing a stronger Core and being more disciplined about their market growth.

STEP 20

1. Segway… where to begin? They built a product in secret and launched it to great fanfare without considering a wide range of questions. How does the product fit into the customer's existing routine—or does it? Can a Segway be used on a sidewalk or on a road without regulators

clamping down over concerns that sidewalk use is unsafe to other pedestrians, and road use is unsafe to both cars and Segway operators? Is the price too high? Perhaps most important, will anyone want to be seen on a Segway, or will users be viewed as "dorky" by others? Paul Graham wrote on his website, "They had focus groups aplenty, I'm sure, but they didn't have the people yelling insults out of cars."

STEP 24

1. One example is the Web browser Netscape, which was the first widely used browser that showed the world how exciting the Internet could be. They were eventually copied by others, most prominently Microsoft. Another example is VisiCalc, the original spreadsheet program from Software Arts, which revolutionized how people used computers—until the lack of a defensible Core prompted Lotus to develop a competing product that reaped the lion's share of the market—which Microsoft then subsequently dominated with Excel. That is why some people call it "first mover disadvantage" instead of "first mover advantage," because it is easy to be first in a market but not be ready to dominate that market long term.

2. One example is the Apple Macintosh, which after stumbling into its "accidental beachhead" of the desktop publishing market, was able to leverage the high word of mouth in the creative professional community to deliver additional valuable and unique products to this market, cementing the association of Apple computers with high-quality products for creative professionals. The features of the Macintosh, such as pixel-addressable computing instead of the more efficient text-only operating systems, would not have made sense in existing markets, so by developing this Beachhead Market in desktop publishing, they were able to dominate a new market. Even after Microsoft gained a giant share of the desktop computing market in the 1990s, Apple's follow-on products were consistently viewed as essential to creative professionals. Another example is the Honda Motor Company. When I first saw Honda products, they were making small mopeds and weed whackers with small motors. After success in this small market, they moved up to larger automobiles, and today they are well known as a luxury automobile manufacturer and are moving into airplanes and sophisticated robots.

INDEX

A

A/B testing: primary market research using, 30; set pricing and use of, 172. *See also* Test Key Assumptions step

Acquisition. *See* Customer acquisition

Advertising business model, 163

Agreement on the Beachhead Market Selection Worksheet, 45

Airbnb, 12

Alba, Jessica, 69

Amazon: Beachhead Market of, 155; Jeff Bezos's use of empty chair customer representation at, 68; low COCA maintained by, 202; Windows of Opportunity and Triggers application by, 146

Amie Street, 162

Apple: Beachhead Market of, 42; competitive positioning by, 122

Ardrey, Jillian, 196

Ariely, Dan, 172

Assumptions: Identify Key Assumptions step, 209–213; Test Key Assumptions step, 215–220

Automobile companies: identify business model of, 165; paying customers acquisition by, 137

Axis to Measure Value Proposition Worksheet, 98–99

B

B2B Process to Acquire a Paying Customer, 137

Bain & Company, 227

Beachhead Markets: brainstorming to identify, 12–14; building End User Profile for the, 47–52; description of a, 154; estimating TAM (Total Addressable Market) for the, 53–63; narrowing your potential, 15–16; primary market research and Market Segmentation Matrix Version 1.0 on, 17–19; Product Plan development for, 231–237; Profile the Persona for the, 65–78; selecting a, 39–45; Top Target Markets to Consider for My Startup form, 16; World War II example of, 42, 154

Beehive student project: Identify Key Assumptions step on the, 211; Test Key Assumptions step on the, 217

Bezos, Jeff, 68

Bias: confirmation, 25–26; selection, 26; social acceptability, 26

Blank, Steve, 23

Blogs, 28

Bottom-Up TAM analysis: Bottom-Up TAM Analysis Worksheet, 62–63; description of, 61

Brainstorming: Idea/Technology, 6, 8; key points related to effective, 6; Market Segmentation, 12–14

Brainstorming forms: Brainstorming What My Startup Will Do, 14; Idea/Technology Brainstorming Notes, 7

BuildLine platform: description of project for building, 74; Profile the Persona for the Beachhead Market illustration for, 75; three Persona Profiles for multisided end user market for, 76–78